Inventory of High Elevation Breeding Birds at Carlsbad Caverns National Park

Natural Resource Data Series NPS/CHDN/NRDS—2012/314

Author:

Steve West
Borderlands Environmental Education and Research Consortium, Inc.
1105 Ocotillo Canyon
Carlsbad, NM 88220

Editors:

M. Hildegard Reiser and Nina Chambers
National Park Service
Chihuahuan Desert Inventory & Monitoring Program
Las Cruces, New Mexcio

Ann Lewis
Physical Science Laboratory
New Mexico State University
Las Cruces, New Mexico

Project Contact:

M. Hildegard Reiser
National Park Service
Chihuahuan Desert Network
New Mexico State University
MSC 3ARP
Las Cruces, New Mexico 88003

April 2012

U.S. Department of the Interior
National Park Service
Natural Resource Stewardship and Science
Fort Collins, Colorado

The National Park Service, Natural Resource Stewardship and Science office in Fort Collins, Colorado publishes a range of reports that address natural resource topics of interest and applicability to a broad audience in the National Park Service and others in natural resource management, including scientists, conservation and environmental constituencies, and the public.

The Natural Resource Data Series is intended for the timely release of basic data sets and data summaries. Care has been taken to assure accuracy of raw data values, but a thorough analysis and interpretation of the data has not been completed. Consequently, the initial analyses of data in this report are provisional and subject to change.

All manuscripts in the series receive the appropriate level of peer review to ensure that the information is scientifically credible, technically accurate, appropriately written for the intended audience, and designed and published in a professional manner.

This report received informal peer review by subject-matter experts who were not directly involved in the collection, analysis, or reporting of the data, and whose background and expertise put them on par technically and scientifically with the authors of the information.

Views, statements, findings, conclusions, recommendations, and data in this report are those of the author(s) and do not necessarily reflect views and policies of the National Park Service, U.S. Department of the Interior. Mention of trade names or commercial products does not constitute endorsement or recommendation for use by the National Park Service.

This report is available from http://science.nature.nps.gov/im/units/chdn/reportpubs.cfm and the Natural Resource Publications Management website (http://www.nature.nps.gov/publications/nrmp/).

Please cite this publication as:

West, S. 2012. Inventory of high elevation breeding birds at Carlsbad Caverns National Park. Natural Resource Data Series NPS/CHDN/NRDS—2012/314. National Park Service, Fort Collins, Colorado.

NPS 130/113639, April 2012

Contents

Contents (continued)

Figures

Tables

Photos

Executive Summary

Carlsbad Caverns National Park (NP) contains high elevation areas with mesic vegetation communities that are spatially isolated in a generally arid region. The high elevation areas of the park are remote, rugged, and difficult to access, and have a low visitation rate. Thus, little information has been compiled on the presence, distribution, or relative abundance of high country breeding birds in the park. This stands in stark contrast with lowland areas such as Rattlesnake Springs, a desert riparian oasis that is heavily birded and from which over 300 species have been recorded.

Studies in Guadalupe Mountains NP and adjacent portions of Lincoln National Forest provide some clues as to what might be expected in this high elevation study. Until the many remote canyons are inventoried, however, the park will not have a complete perspective of the true status of endangered, threatened or species of concern.

In this survey, 1,524 individuals from 50 species were detected on point counts, plus an additional six species were recorded between survey points or on scouting trips before or after the survey date. Active nests were found of White-winged Dove, Mourning Dove, Cassin's Kingbird, Gray Vireo, Plumbeous Vireo, Northern Mockingbird, and Phainopepla. Nest-defense, dependent young, or other strong nest-associated behavior was noted in Say's Phoebe, Ash-throated Flycatcher, Rock Wren, Bewick's Wren, Blue-gray Gnatcatcher, Canyon Towhee, Rufous-crowned Sparrow, Varied Bunting, and Scott's Oriole. Because of the time constraints of the survey, an aggressive search for nests was not possible. Hot, midday conditions generally were present at the completion of the survey, and the PI did not want to disturb birds unduly at that time of day.

The summer 2003 surveys added one species (Elf Owl) to the park's bird list, provided a second record (since 1943) of a species once thought extirpated (Montezuma Quail), and added to the knowledge of nesting species in areas of the park rarely visited, including two state threatened species (Gray Vireo and Varied Bunting). First nesting records of Gray Vireo and Plumbeous Vireo also were established.

Introduction

Carlsbad Caverns National Park (NP) contains high elevation areas with mesic vegetation communities that are spatially isolated in a generally arid region. The high elevation areas of the park are remote, rugged, and difficult to access, and have a low visitation rate. Thus, little information has been compiled on the presence, distribution, or relative abundance of high country breeding birds in the park. This stands in stark contrast with lowland areas such as Rattlesnake Springs, a desert riparian oasis that is heavily birded and from which over 300 species have been recorded.

Studies in Guadalupe Mountains NP and adjacent portions of Lincoln National Forest provide some clues as to what might be expected in this high elevation study. Until the many remote canyons are inventoried, however, the park will not have a complete perspective of the true status of endangered, threatened or species of concern including Montezuma Quail, Mexican Spotted Owl, Gray Vireo, and Varied Bunting.

Methods

Six areas were selected for this investigation based primarily on elevation that generally ranged between 1,280 m to 1,890 m. These six study sites were over the western half of Carlsbad Caverns NP (Figure 1), the least known portion of the park as far as birds are concerned. Each study area was visited twice from May 2003 through early July 2003 with at least seven days between visits at the same site.

Each site generally ran either on a ridge top or a canyon bottom. Each route consisted of 14 sampling sites (except Yucca Mesa) with 200 to 250 meters between sites. Each survey route followed a roughly linear arrangement. Data were recorded on Point Count Data Forms.

Each survey started at about 0530 and proceeded to the end point. At each point, the Principal Investigator (PI) recorded bird presence through a variety of categories including typical detection, flyovers, juveniles, and flushed. Upon arriving at each point, the PI waited for one minute before recording data to allow the birds to settle down.

Once the minute passed, birds were recorded in the first 0-3 minute time period. This was broken down into 0-50 m, greater than 50 m, associated flyovers, and individual flyovers. Birds were recorded in each column during this time period. After the 0-3 minute time period, the same information was collected from 3-5 minutes.

Information on each site was entered with other data relating to the site into a Trimble GeoExplorer3 GPS receiver. This included information on station identification (ID), slope, aspect, dominant landform, dominant understory and overstory vegetation, maximum tree height, and brush and herbaceous layer height. This generally was done by the PI on a walk of the route on the day before the survey or by an assistant on the day of the survey.

Any other information on the site was recorded in the field notes to include bird activity, other wildlife observed, and each site was photographed.

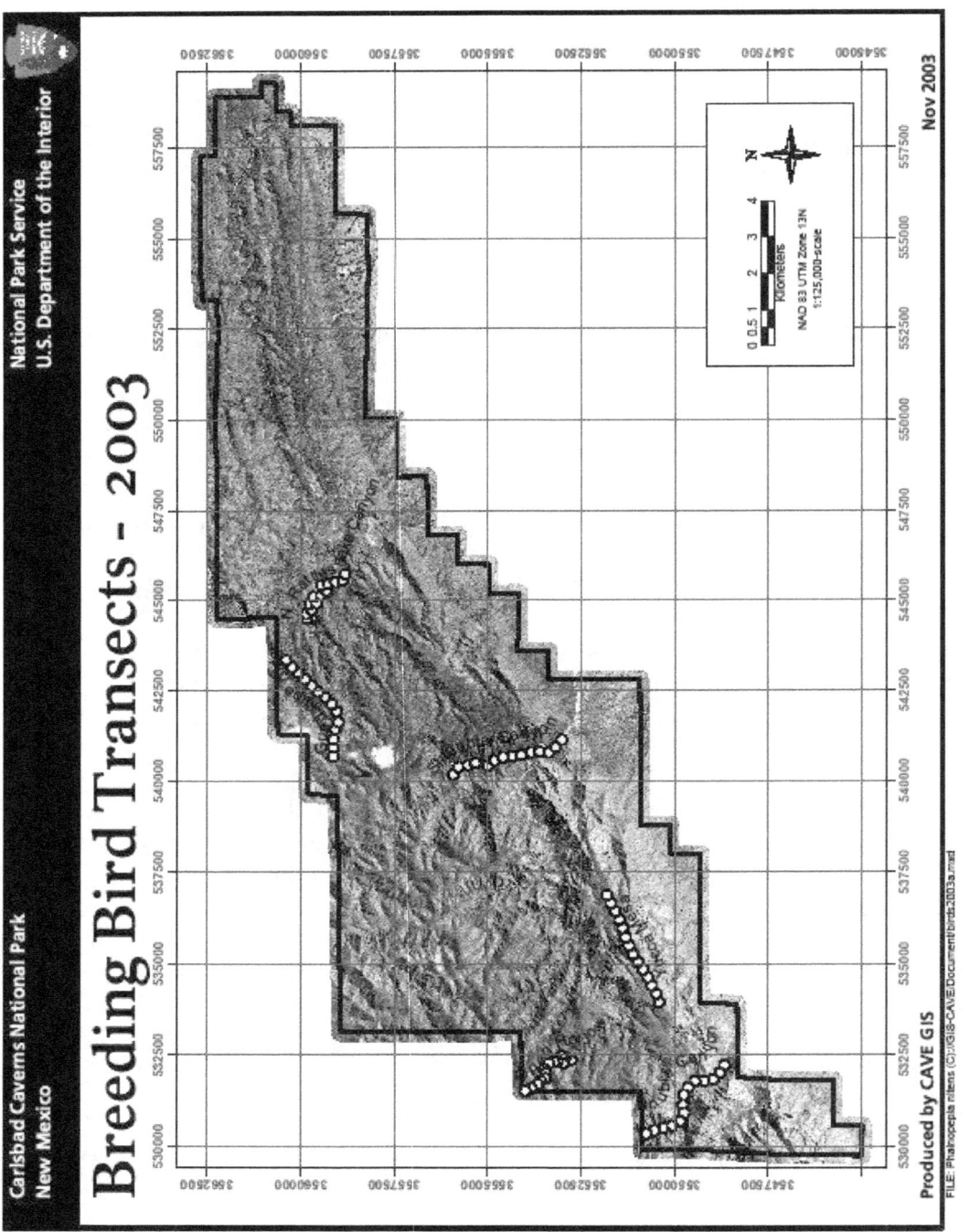

Figure 1. Breeding bird transects at Carlsbad Caverns NP, 2003.

2

Results

Dates, locations, and times of surveys are presented by study area in Table 1. A complete list of bird species observed, including scientific names is presented in Appendix A. All common and scientific bird names follow the 7th edition of the Check-list of North American Birds (AOU 1998, 2011) and species code follow Pyle and DeSante (2003). The common and scientific names of plants are listed in Appendix B. Survey route maps and locations of each point count are provided in Appendixes C and D. The survey route maps are in chronological order by first date visited.

Table 1. Breeding bird surveys in Carlsbad Caverns NP, 2003.

Date	Area	Duration
May 3	North Slaughter Canyon	0534-0925
May 25	Rattlesnake Canyon	0536-0836
June 2	Yucca Mesa	0530-0824
June 6	Guadalupe Ridge	0542-0814
June 10	North Slaughter Canyon	0530-0827
June 13	Open Hollow Gulch	0530-0822
June 20	North Double Canyon	0533-0821
June 24	Guadalupe Ridge	0540-0815
June 26	Open Hollow Gulch	0530-0811
June 29	Yucca Mesa	0530-0833
June 30	Rattlesnake Canyon	0530-0821
July 3	North Double Canyon	0530-0819

North Slaughter Canyon
Thirty-five species were found on this survey route.

Expectations
Of all the areas surveyed during the summer of 2003, North Slaughter Canyon (NSC) was the only one in which some information on the site was found in the literature. This was mainly because Cave Swallow (*Petrochelidon fulva*) colonies and other species in the canyon were reported by observers. Because this route passes three of the best known back-country caves that hold Cave Swallow populations (Ogle, Goat, and Lake), there are data on this area dating back to 1930.

The first half of NSC surveyed was largely broad, large-cobbled canyon bottom. After that point, the canyon tightened up and much of the route followed trails on benches. Though extensive cliffs exist in the canyon, most of them were too far away to impact the survey (in terms of lighting conditions, difficulty in making observations, etc.). The PI has been up this canyon about two dozen times in all seasons except fall.

This canyon was already known to have a Gray Vireo (*Vireo vicinior*) population (of undetermined size), and it was assumed that Varied Bunting (*Passerina versicolor*) might nest here also.

Vegetation

Vegetation changed somewhat from the first to the second half of the survey route. One characteristic throughout was the presence of thick stands of *Acacia* spp. and, to a lesser degree, honey mesquite (*Prosopis glandulosa*) on the adjoining benches, probably a holdover from grazing decades ago. The canyon bottom was populated mostly by Apache plume (*Fallugia paradoxa*), lechuguilla (*Agave lechuguilla*), sotol (*Dasylirion* spp.), cholla (*Cylindropuntia* spp.), and New Mexico prickly pear (*Opuntia phaeacantha*) with scattered deciduous trees and bushes including little walnut (*Juglans microcarpa*), Texas madrone (*Arbutus xalapensis*), Mexican buckeye (*Ungnadia speciosa*), and sumac (*Rhus* spp.). After that point, there were more gray oak (*Quercus grisea*) and thicker stands of *Acacia* spp. Little walnut was found within a few meters of almost every survey point.

Survey Details

The survey route through NSC was run on May 3rd by the PI and Renee West and on June 10th by the PI. On both occasions the survey was begun on the day of the survey by hiking before dawn to the beginning point and starting at the scheduled time, being only a short distance from the parking area to the first survey point. On both occasions the PI did not go beyond Stop 14. Photos were taken on each of the survey points (Appendix E).

On the first survey (May 3rd), 31 species were detected (Table 2), including Gray Vireo, Hammond's Flycatcher (*Empidonax hammondii*), and Blue-gray Gnatcatcher (*Polioptila caerulea*) from an off-survey site. The number of individuals recorded were 199, including 40 seen off the survey points. On June 10th only 26 species were found including those off route—Turkey Vulture (*Cathartes aura*), Elf Owl (*Micrathene whitneyi*), Western Kingbird (*Tyrannus verticalis*), Blue-gray Gnatcatcher, and Black-chinned Sparrow (*Spizella atrogularis*). On this second trip, 342 individuals were found including 173 seen off-route. This represented a decrease in species of 19% from the first to second survey and an increase in individuals of 72%. When the large number of Cave Swallows seen exiting Goat Cave between survey points are removed (108), the number of total individuals observed was more similar between the two survey dates (199 in May versus 234 in June). On both occasions the weather was hot and dry and bird activity had largely ended by the end of the survey.

Eight species detected on the first survey were not seen on the second—White-winged Dove (*Zenaida asiatica*), Black-chinned Hummingbird (*Archilochus alexandri*), Hammond's Flycatcher, Gray Flycatcher (*Empidonax wrightii*), Say's Phoebe (*Sayornis saya*), Phainopepla (*Phainopepla nitens*), Spotted Towhee (*Pipilo maculates*), and Bullock's Oriole (*Icterus bullockii*). Four species detected on the second survey were not observed on the first one—Yellow-billed Cuckoo (*Coccyzus americanus*), Elf Owl, Western Kingbird, and Black-chinned Sparrow. Three species were not detected at point count stations—Elf Owl, Hammond's Flycatcher, and Western Kingbird (Table 3).

Table 2. Species detected at point count stations for both sampling dates (birds listed taxonomically).

	NORTH SLAUGHTER CANYON		RATTLESNAKE CANYON		YUCCA MESA		GUADALUPE RIDGE		OPEN HOLLOW GULCH		NORTH DOUBLE CANYON		TOTAL
	5/3/2003	6/10/2003	5/25/2003	6/30/2003	6/2/2003	6/29/2003	6/6/2003	6/24/2003	6/13/2003	6/26/2003	6/20/2003	7/3/2003	
TUVU	9		1	1	1	1	1	1	1				16
RTHA							1						1
GOEA			1										1
AMKE												1	1
SCQU	2	5	1	2			2	2					14
WWDO	3			1							6		10
MODO	8	9	9	1	2	12	2		14	13	2	2	74
YBCU		1								2			3
GHOW	1												1
CONI			2	1		1	1	7					12
COPO	3				1		1	1			2		8
WTSW								2	1		1		4
BCHU	1					1							2
ACWO						1							1
LBWO	2	5	7	3	1	3		3	6	7	1		38
WEWP			1		1				10	3	1		16
COFL									9	6			15
SAPH	1					1							2
ATFL	16	26	3	2	4	2		5	2	2	17	1	80
CAKI					20	23		3	13	41			100
GRVI	2	9	15	17	13	18		2	6	12	19	23	136
PLVI					1				30	22			53
VGSW					3				1				4
CASW	45	19		1	1	8		2			19	23	118
BUSH										2			2
CACW	8	7											15
ROWR	4	2	10	10	3	21	1	6	2	3	8	11	81
CNWR	1	13	7	27		6			1	8	26	17	106
BEWR	2	10	5	5	3	9	3	3	6	22	15	16	99
HETH			2										2

Table 2. Species detected at point count stations for both sampling dates (continued).

	NORTH SLAUGHTER CANYON		RATTLESNAKE CANYON		YUCCA MESA		GUADALUPE RIDGE		OPEN HOLLOW GULCH		NORTH DOUBLE CANYON		TOTAL
	5/3/2003	6/10/2003	5/25/2003	6/30/2003	6/2/2003	6/29/2003	6/6/2003	6/24/2003	6/13/2003	6/26/2003	6/20/2003	7/3/2003	
NOMO	35	55	39	56	47	24	15	58	29	6	8	6	378
PHAI	4		1										5
HETA			5	2	6	2	4		17	19	17	5	77
WETA										1	1		2
SPTO	1			1		1			20	12	17	15	66
CANT	1	1	1			3	3	2			2	1	15
RCSP	1	5	6	10	1	3	8	8	3	4	5	22	76
BCSP					2	1			1	4	1	4	13
BTSP	2	3	7				1	2					15
BLGR	3	31	19	22	3	14	14	4	3	5	40	29	187
VABU	1	1	4	3							2	2	13
BHCO	1	2	2			2			1				8
BUOR	1												1
SCOR	9	38	20	15	15	8	5	1	10	3	11	33	168
HOFI	8	10	6	1	5	1	1		8	3	1		44
UNK	1		1										2
TOTAL	176	252	175	181	133	166	62	112	194	200	222	212	2,085

6

Table 3. Species not detected at point count stations but observed in between stations or off route in the transect area.

	NORTH SLAUGHTER CANYON	RATTLE-SNAKE CANYON	YUCCA MESA	GUADALUPE RIDGE	OPEN HOLLOW GULCH	NORTH DOUBLE CANYON
MONQ			X			
BTPI			X			
ELOW	X					
LENI		X				
BTHH					X	
OSFL			X			
HAFL	X					
GRFL					X	
WEKI	X					
BGGN			X			
BHGR						X

Results and Discussion

The following comments apply to species detected on the North Slaughter Canyon route:

<u>Yellow-billed Cuckoo</u>: A single individual was seen and photographed on June 10th at Stop 12 (Photo 1). This species probably nests in the area. It also was detected in another dry canyon, Open Hollow Gulch, later in the summer. As this species is a late migrant, it would not have been expected here in the early May survey.

Photo 1. Yellow-billed Cuckoo at Stop 12, North Slaughter Canyon on June 10th.

Elf Owl: The first park record was of one flushed from Little Walnut, Stop 5. This species was only recently recorded in the Guadalupe Mountains in 1994. Another individual was found at the end of July near the mouth of Rattlesnake Canyon by Daniel Moen.

Hammond's Flycatcher: The single individual seen on May 3rd was a migrant and not a species expected to nest at this low elevation.

Gray Flycatcher: The single individual seen at Stop 13 on May 3rd was a migrating individual and not a nesting species. This species was detected on other surveys and probably nests at higher elevations in the Guadalupe Mountains.

Western Kingbird: There was an unusual sighting of a single bird near Stop 3 on June 10th. Whether it was a wandering late migrant or one attempting to nest was never determined. The bird gave the Western Kingbird call and had the white outer tail feathers.

Gray Vireo: This species has been known from Slaughter Canyon for many years. What was not known was the extent of the population. Although the various branches of Slaughter Canyon covers an extensive area, we now have an idea of what is found in the area surveyed, and it is likely that the other branches have similar densities. On the first survey, it was found only on two stops (single individuals) with three others noted between stops. On the second survey, which was closer to their nesting period, the species was found on 6 of the 14 stops. Based on this, it appears that probably a minimum of six or seven nesting pairs were in the area surveyed. This species is listed as a threatened species by the New Mexico Department of Game and Fish.

Phainopepla: Seen only on the May survey when pairs were found at Stops 5 and 9, and a nest was located at Stop 5. Not seen on the June survey.

Spotted Towhee: One individual seen on the May survey was undoubtedly a migrating bird. This species nests at much higher elevations in the Guadalupe Mountains.

Bullock's Oriole: A single male was seen on May 3rd at Stop 14 and was undoubtedly a migrant bird. There is no appropriate nesting habitat for this species in Slaughter Canyon.

Varied Bunting: Varied buntings were seen on both surveys, with there probably being only one nesting pair present. It is unclear why more were not sighted, although in some years this species is active later in the summer and both of these surveys were done early in the season. This species is listed as threatened by the New Mexico Department of Game and Fish.

Rattlesnake Canyon

Twenty-eight species were detected on this survey route.

Expectations

The portions of Rattlesnake Canyon surveyed were mostly large cobbled limestone bottoms with sloping escarpments gradually leading up from the canyon bottom. A few cliffs were significant in size but some had broad benches at the base of them. Some prior work had been done on birds in Rattlesnake Canyon but mostly during the winter in conjunction with Christmas Bird Counts. The only time the PI had been in the canyon in the past had been at that time of year (late

December to early January). Nothing appears in the New Mexico Ornithological Society Field Notes that refers to Rattlesnake Canyon.

Except for the upper portions of North Double Canyon, this is the narrowest overall canyon surveyed during the summer of 2003. Based on what was found elsewhere in the park in previous years it was thought that this canyon would probably have populations of Gray Vireo and perhaps Varied Bunting.

Vegetation

Most of the canyon bottom was open with scattered deciduous trees along the edges of the drainage. Few ponderosa pine (*Pinus ponderosa*) were noted and most were seen beyond Stop 11. The canyon bottoms had mostly gray oak, little walnut, mescal bean (*Sophora secundiflora*), and sotol. Lower densities of banana yucca (*Yucca baccata*), alligator juniper (*Juniperus deppeana*), Mexican buckeye, and one-seed juniper (*Juniperus monosperma*) were observed. Rocky Mountain maple (*Acer glabrum*) also occurred in low numbers with more individuals seen above Stop 6.

Survey Details

The survey route through Rattlesnake Canyon was run on two occasions, May 25th and June30[th]. On the first survey, the PI was accompanied by Renee West. On both occasions the survey began by hiking before dawn to the beginning point and starting at the scheduled time. On both occasions, because of the heat, the PI went only a short distance beyond Stop 14. Photographs of each of the 14 survey points are found in Appendix F.

On the first survey (May 25th), 26 species were detected (Table 2) including Lesser Nighthawk (*Chordeiles acutipennis*) and Common Poorwill (*Phalaenoptilus nuttallii*), which were calling before the time allowed for the first stop. An unidentified hummingbird was noted, probably a Black-chinned. One hundred thirty-three (133) individuals were recorded plus an additional 31 between route stops. The second survey, run on June 30th, found 21 species, including Common Poorwill again before the start time of the survey at Stop 1. One hundred sixty-six (166) individuals were detected with 44 found between stops. A comparison of the two surveys showed a reduction by 19% in the number of species, but an increase of 1.2% in the number of individuals. Weather on both trips was very warm and dry.

Eight species were detected on the first survey but not located on the second one—Golden Eagle (*Aquila chrysaetos*), Lesser Nighthawk, the unidentified hummingbird, Western Wood-Pewee (*Contopus sordidulus*), Hermit Thrush (*Catharus guttatus*), Phainopepla, Black-throated Sparrow (*Amphispiza bilineata*), and Brown-headed Cowbird (*Molothrus ater*). On the second survey, only White-winged Dove and Cave Swallow were recorded as new to the count. Only one species, Lesser Nighthawk was not detected at a point count station (Table 3).

Results and Discussion

The following comments apply to species detected on the Rattlesnake Canyon route.

Golden Eagle: The only one seen during the summer 2003 surveys was a single adult in Rattlesnake Canyon as a flyover at Stop 5.

White-winged Dove: Although the following species were encountered frequently on the surveys, only one White-winged Dove was detected and that was at Stop 14 on the second survey. The species apparently occurs in low density through most of the canyons in the park.

Mourning Dove (*Zenaida macroura*): Relatively common on the May survey (8 of 14 stops), the species was largely absent by the second survey in late June (found on only 1 of 14 stops).

Lesser Nighthawk: The status of this species in the park, away from the open lowlands, is not clear. One was heard calling clearly prior to the start time on Stop 1 on May 25th. The PI knows of no other records for the canyon bottoms.

Western Wood-Pewee: This species is often a late migrant in the area so observing only one in late May (or even into the first week in June) is not unusual.

Gray Vireo: This species was found throughout the canyon in lower numbers than in other canyons, yet widespread. Six birds were recorded on the May survey and 16 were found in late June. The late June birds were much more active, and three nests were found including one photographed on the nest (Photo 2). Prior to this summer, an actual nesting record did not exist of this species for the park. They seemed scarce at the beginning of the survey and were more frequent as one progressed up the canyon.

The Guadalupe Ridge survey also found them singing from the northern extremes of Rattlesnake Canyon. Using the number found at the end of June, it is estimated that a minimum of five, and maybe six, nesting pairs inhabit the canyon. This is probably a very conservative number as three nests were found with very little time spent actually searching for them. This species is state listed as threatened by the New Mexico Department of Game and Fish.

Photo 2. Gray Vireo on nest in Rattlesnake Canyon at Stop 10, June 30, 2003.

Hermit Thrush: The single bird singing at Stop 1 on May 29th was undoubtedly a late migrant.

Northern Mockingbird (*Mimus polyglottos*): Widespread and on both surveys by far the most common species heard in the canyon. Out of 28 stops on the two surveys, Northern Mockingbird was found on 26 of the stops for an average of over 2.6 birds per stop.

Phainopepla: This bird was seen only on the late May survey when it was probably nesting in the canyon. After the nesting season this bird often disappears from southeastern New Mexico.

Hepatic Tanager (*Piranga flava*): When a group of five was found at Stop 8 on May 29th, it was thought that they must be late migrants. The species also was found in lower numbers up the canyon at the end of June and detected from Guadalupe Ridge into the upper reaches of Rattlesnake Canyon. Prior to this summer, it was thought that this species only occurred in ponderosa pine forest higher in the Guadalupe Mountains.

Varied Bunting: Seen on both surveys with four or five pairs present. On the second survey, three were seen at route stops, and an additional four were detected between stops. Although most of the individuals seen were singing males perched on top of sotol stalks (Photo 3), a female also was seen at Stop 8. She was probably nesting in the immediate area based on her behavior. No attempt was made to find the nest considering the delicate status of this species in the state. The only nest of this species ever found in New Mexico was in Walnut Canyon in 1972. This species is listed as threatened by the New Mexico Department of Game and Fish.

Photo 3. Varied Bunting on sotol stalk at Stop 13, June 30, 2003. An individual was also seen singing from this spot on the May survey.

Yucca Mesa

Thirty-three species were found on this survey route.

Expectations

Yucca Mesa is high elevation grassland with scattered pine and juniper. The large flat area is bordered on one side by the eastern face of the Guadalupe escarpment and the other by West Slaughter Canyon. Though in a few places the mesa is narrow, in most areas it is broad enough to support a variety of plant and animal life. No narrow ridges exist along the transect line. It is one of the few areas in the park with an extensive area of grassland.

This area has been visited on numerous occasions in the past to check on bird numbers, usually in conjunction with Christmas Bird Counts when one would expect a somewhat different suite of species. The PI has been on the mesa on numerous occasions, but always in winter or spring, never in summer. A search of field notes from the New Mexico Ornithological Society reveals no records reported from the summer months.

Due to the presence of extensive grassland, it was thought there might be some more typical grassland species such as Horned Larks (*Eremophila alpestris*) and meadowlarks (*Sturnella* spp.), but neither was found. The shrub encroachment may be reducing the likelihood of obligate grassland bird species being present.

Vegetation

Yucca Mesa is a broad, mostly flat area covered largely with grasses. There are scattering of alligator juniper and ponderosa pine at the beginning and at the end of the transect. Scattered across the mesa are sotol, New Mexico prickly pear, and a few mountain mahogany (*Cercocarpus* spp.). This site, along with Guadalupe Ridge, seems to have the lowest diversity of plant life.

Survey Details

Yucca Mesa was the only route with 13 stops, because there was not enough area for a 14th stop due to the length of the mesa. The survey route on Yucca Mesa was run on two occasions, June 2nd and June 29th. On June 1st, Renee West and the PI hiked up in late evening, arriving near Stop 1 on the transect well after dark. The researchers listened for owls and nightjars (Caprimulgids) and began the survey the following morning. No owls were detected. On June 28th, the PI repeated the same route, but was not accompanied by anyone else.

Some birds of interest were found in Yucca Canyon on the walk down after completing the Yucca Mesa transect. Photos were taken on each of the Yucca Mesa survey points, except Stops 6 and 12 (Appendix G).

On the first survey (June 2nd), 26 species were found (Table 2), including those found in Yucca Canyon. Counting only birds on the survey, 21 species were found at the survey points and two more species—Montezuma Quail (*Cyrtonyx montezumae*) and Canyon Wren (*Catherpes mexicanus*)—were detected between points. One hundred and five (105) individuals were found, plus 66 found between points and an additional 16 in the canyon on the hike down. The second survey was run on June 29th. Twenty-nine species were observed (including one species found in Yucca Canyon and four species seen away from the survey points: Band-tailed Pigeon (*Patagioenas fasciata*), Common Poorwill, Western Wood-Pewee, and Blue-gray Gnatcatcher.

Restricting the count to only the species seen on the transect 21 were found on June 2nd and 23 species on June 29th, a difference of less than 10%. Individuals on the second survey were similar with 122 seen on the survey points (versus 105 on June 2nd), 55 off-survey points on June 29th (versus 66 on June 2nd). Species counts and number of individuals also differed for Yucca Canyon, more species and individuals were observed on June 29th (13 species and 35 individuals) than on June 2nd (8 species and 16 individuals).

Three species found on June 2nd were not found on June 29th: Montezuma Quail, Common Poorwill, and Olive-sided Flycatcher (*Contopus cooperi*). Five species were found on June 29th, but not on the earlier survey: Band-tailed Pigeon, Black-chinned Hummingbird, Say's Phoebe, Spotted Towhee, and Brown-headed Cowbird. The highest number of species not detected at point count stations was the Yucca Mesa transect (Table 3).

Results and Discussion
The following comments apply to species detected on the Yucca Mesa route and on the return hike through Yucca Canyon. The PI did not go past Stop 14, although a few other individual birds were detected after the end of the survey time and before returning to camp.

Montezuma Quail: At dawn on the morning of June 2nd as the PI was approaching Stop 4, a single Montezuma Quail was heard to give its call three times. That area is a combination of scattered ponderosa pine, short oak, and grasses. A brief search was made for the bird at the end of the survey route and a couple of hours later. Another search was conducted on June 29th, but nothing was found. No tracks, feathers, or characteristic dig marks were located.

Band-tailed Pigeon: Upon returning to the campsite after finishing the survey on June 29th, one of the field crew saw a single Band-tailed Pigeon fly overhead. This was the only one detected during the summer, although in the past, they have summered (and probably nested) in nearby Slaughter Canyon.

Acorn Woodpecker (*Melanerpes formicivorus*): The only one detected was one at Stop 3 on the June 29th survey. This is one of the few reliable places in the park for this species. Previous to this survey, all the records had been from winter months.

Olive-sided Flycatcher: One late migrant was seen at Stop 14 on June 2nd. This species is a late migrant in the spring and has been recorded at lowland elevations, such as Rattlesnake Springs, into the second week of June. Nothing is really known about movements of migrants in high elevation.

Gray Vireo: This species was surprisingly widespread on the mesa, and was also observed in Yucca Canyon and on the escarpment face. Nine pairs of Gray Vireos were detected on June 2nd and as many as 11 on June 29th. An additional two pairs were found in Yucca Canyon. A range of 10-12 pairs of Gray Vireo is evident from the trailhead to the end of the survey route. Some of the calling birds detected on this route were actually calling from the adjacent escarpment. This species is state listed as a threatened species by the New Mexico Department of Game and Fish.

Plumbeous Vireo (*Vireo plumbeus*): Only one was found in the stand of ponderosa pine at the beginning of the route on June 2nd. It was not found again and may have been a late migrant.

Northern Mockingbird: This species was virtually everywhere on the first survey (seen on all 14 stops plus 12 between points), but none in Yucca Canyon. On the second survey, mockingbirds were seen on 12 of 14 stops with 23 individuals plus 6 between points and 4 in Yucca Canyon.

Rufous-crowned Sparrow (*Aimophila ruficeps*): This sparrow species was scarce despite what seemed to be appropriate habitat. This species was only seen on one of the stops on the first trip (but eight additional birds were detected between stops) and found on only three of the stops on the second trip. This species also was present in Yucca Canyon.

Black-chinned Sparrow: Black-chinned Sparrows were found in similar numbers to Rufous-crowned Sparrows. The status of this species is difficult to determine because of the apparent and shifting densities of this species.

Varied Bunting: This species was not present on the mesa nor heard from the adjoining escarpment on West Slaughter Canyon. On both return trips, however, a male was seen singing in Yucca Canyon about half-way down the canyon. It was undoubtedly nesting in the same area.

Guadalupe Ridge
Twenty-four species were found on the Guadalupe Ridge survey route.

Expectations
Guadalupe Ridge is a high elevation area in the north side of Carlsbad Caverns National Park, and it is a largely exposed site. The route runs along the top of a ridge and the habitat is uniform throughout the route. It was not expected to have the same potential for diversity that is found in canyon bottoms. Because the area is largely open and might harbor a different variety of grassland-shrub species, this ridge was an appropriate area to survey. Additionally, a pair of Montezuma Quail was found just beyond the survey end point a few years ago, the first record for the park since 1943. Because of the interesting distribution and declining populations of this species throughout its range, it would be good to see if the species might still be found along this ridge.

Vegetation
The vegetation on this exposed ridge showed little variety from the beginning to the end of the survey transect. One sandstone outcrop at Stop 9 showed numerous soaptree yucca (*Yucca elata*), Heyder's nipple cactus (*Mammillaria heyderi*), and cane cholla (*Cylindropuntia spinosior*), which were not noted elsewhere on the route. Otherwise, the survey showed scattered juniper species, mountain mahogany, New Mexico prickly pear, and some oaks (*Quercus* spp.). Grasses were widespread but were not identified.

Survey Details
The survey route on Guadalupe Ridge was run on two occasions, June 6th and June 24th. On both occasions the field crew camped near the beginning point of the survey, ran the survey early the next morning, returned to the campsite, and left the field by about noon. On the first survey, the PI was accompanied by David Roemer and Sara Swann, and on the second trip by Donna Laing and David Roemer. Photos were taken on each of the survey points (Appendix H).

On the first survey (June 6th), only 16 species were found (Table 2). Three of these were seen between route points, Red-tailed Hawk (*Buteo jamaicensis*), Cave Swallow, and Canyon Wren.

14

At two of the fourteen sites, only a single bird was seen. Only 49 individuals were found plus an additional 15 between route points. These low numbers were due largely to very high and cold winds and accompanying noise on the ridge that morning. Weather conditions were much improved on the second survey (June 24th). Twenty-one species were found with only one of those being seen between survey points. Seventy-seven individuals were found plus an additional 16 seen between survey points. Because of better weather conditions, the second survey showed an increase of over 30% in species and almost 44% in the number of individuals.

Only two species were found on the first survey but missed on the second—Hepatic Tanager and House Finch (*Carpodacus mexicanus*). Eight species were found on the second survey but not the first, including Mourning Dove, Common Poorwill, White-throated Swift (*Aeronautes saxatalis*), Ladder-backed Woodpecker (*Picoides scalaris*), Say's Phoebe, Ash-throated Flycatcher (*Myiarchis cinerascens*), Cassin's Kingbird (*Tyrannus vociferans*), and Gray Vireo. There were no species detected on this transect that had not been observed at a point count station (Table 3).

Results and Discussion
The following comments apply to species detected on the Guadalupe Ridge route.

White-throated Swift: On June 24th two White-throated Swifts were found at Stop 13. Because very few nesting locations for this species are known, it would be interesting to identify where the nearest nesting colony is located. The only known colony in the park is in West Slaughter Canyon in Window Cave about 7.2 km to the southwest. Undoubtedly, other colonies of this species exist in the park.

Gray Vireo: This species is listed as threatened by the New Mexico Department of Game and Fish. Probably because of the high winds on June 6th, none were detected. On June 24th, single individuals were heard singing from the slopes in adjacent North Rattlesnake Canyon. Additionally, on June 24th instead of returning to the campsite via the survey route, the PI dropped into the head of Walnut Canyon and returned from that direction. At least eight Gray Vireos were detected in that short stretch of canyon. Although no nests were found, the species undoubtedly nests there and in the adjacent North Rattlesnake Canyon. There are probably a minimum of five or six nesting pairs in those two areas mentioned.

Cave Swallow: This species was seen only twice, once near Stop 13 on June 6th and two over Stop 14 on June 24th. Again, there may be undiscovered colonies of this species in the area, but the nearest known nesting site to these two observations is probably Lake Cave, about 2.8 km south.

Cactus Wren (*Campylorhynchus brunneicapillus*): Not detected on the route, but found on June 24th in upper Walnut Canyon on the return hike. One was found calling loudly from a stand of cane cholla on a wide bench adjacent to the drainage.

Blue-gray Gnatcatcher: This species is found in low numbers in the Guadalupe Mountains and almost exclusively in canyon bottoms. Although not found on the route itself, two were found in upper Walnut Canyon and were, undoubtedly, nesting.Northern Mockingbird: On both surveys, this was the most widespread species. It was found on 6 of 14 stops on June 6th and on all 14 stops on June 24th. On June 6th, Northern Mockingbirds constituted 23% of all individuals, and on June 24th it was 39%.

Hepatic Tanager: Two were detected at Stops 13 and 14 on June 6th. The birds were seen and were also calling. They were not found on June 24th although they probably nest in adjacent upper portions of North Rattlesnake Canyon. The surveys at lower elevations of Rattlesnake Canyon found the species at several sites. Summer Tanagers (*Piranga rubra*) nest in riparian areas at lower (Rattlesnake Springs) and higher elevations (Sitting Bull Falls), whereas Hepatic Tanagers were once thought to be more restricted to higher elevations with ponderosa pine. Detecting the species here and in lower and drier Rattlesnake Canyon indicates that they, at least partially, use dry canyons for nesting.

Varied Bunting: Not detected, but possibly occurring in the upper portions of Walnut Canyon. Varied Bunting is listed as a threatened species by the New Mexico Department of Game and Fish.

Open Hollow Gulch
Thirty-two species were found on this survey route.

Expectations
Open Hollow Gulch (OHG) is a high elevation canyon area in the far western part of the park. The route runs from the park boundary in a southeasterly direction. As with the North Double Canyon survey route, there is nothing in the ornithological literature about this drainage system. Because of this, and the fact that the adjoining sections of national forest land are also poorly studied, there was no idea what to expect.

This canyon is not typical when compared with many of the other canyons surveyed during 2003. This canyon bottom is relatively wide at spots with broad, deep-soiled benches on some sides. Large cobblestone is not always characteristic of the canyon bottom, which is a generally level canyon bottom. A good mix of deciduous and coniferous species occurs with an occasional large clump of deciduous vegetation in the canyon bottom.

Because of the isolation and the canyon characteristics, several species that were considered possible included Mexican Spotted Owl (*Strix occidentalis*), Blue-throated Hummingbird (*Lampornis clemenciae*), and others. The area provided an interesting mix of higher and lower elevation species such as Plumbeous and Gray Vireos discussed below.

Vegetation
The makeup of vegetation through the survey area changed little, only the relatively densities seemed to change. One exception may have been that Rocky Mountain maple was more dominant lower down rather than higher up, probably because of additional water. Overall, the area was characterized by broad, flat benches populated with New Mexico prickly pear, ponderosa pine, gray oak, and sotol. Many of these same plants also grew in the canyon bottom. Stands of mountain mahogany occurred often on the escarpment leading up to the benches. Texas madrone was uncommon, but was found frequently along the canyon wash edges.

A crested cactus was found on the south bend of the canyon between Stops 5 and 6 on June 17, 2003 by one of the field crew (Donna Laing) (Photo 4).

Photo 4. A crested cactus found in OHG between Stops 5 and 6, June 17, 2003. Cresting happens when a new growth emerges from a line rather than a point. It is spontaneous and unpredictable, and no two examples are alike. These mutants tend to be slow-growing.

Survey Details

The survey route on OHG was run on two occasions, June 13th and 26th. On both occasions the field crew hiked from nearby Cottonwood Well on national forest land, over the ridge, and to the park boundary. The first survey point was at the park boundary and continued further into the park from there. On both occasions the field crew arrived the day before the survey and, on June 12th, the PI covered the route in the evening before the survey the next morning. After running the surveys, the field crew left the area about mid-day for the hike back to Cottonwood Well. On both trips the PI was accompanied by Donna Laing and Mike Woolman. Photos were taken on each of the survey points (Appendix I).

On the first survey (June 13th), 30 species were detected (Table 2) including four species that were detected between survey points: Yellow-billed Cuckoo, Gray Flycatcher, Bushtit (*Psaltriparus minimus*), and Blue-gray Gnatcatcher. On both survey days, the PI went about 250 meters beyond the last survey point and, on the first survey day, several additional species were found: Blue-throated Hummingbird, Black-chinned Hummingbird, and Western Tanager (*Piranga ludoviciana*). One hundred forty-eight (148) individuals were found from points 1 to 14, including seven individuals seen away from the points.

The second survey was done on June 26th with similar results. Twenty-six species were found, including two species seen between points (Common Poorwill and Blue-gray Gnatcatcher). As on June 13th, the PI went beyond the last survey point and found two species not seen on the route that day (Turkey Vulture and Cave Swallow). On this date, 153 individuals were found on the route, including 21 individuals found between route points. The weather on both survey days was basically the same with a little more wind on the second survey. The number of species from trip 1 to trip 2 dropped slightly by about 13%, whereas the number of individuals rose even more slightly by 3%.

White-throated Swift, Blue-throated and Black-chinned Hummingbird, Gray Flycatcher, Violet-green Swallow (*Tachycineta thalassina*), and Brown-headed Cowbird were found on the first survey, but not detected on the second. On the second survey only two species were found that were new to the count—Common Poorwill and Cave Swallow. Only Blue-throated Hummingbird, and Gray Flycatcher were not detected at point count stations (Table 3).

Results and Discussion
The following comments apply to species detected on the OHG route and in the area directly beyond the route.

Yellow-billed Cuckoo: This species was heard between Stops 7 and 8 on June 13th and seen at Stop 7 on June 26th; it was likely nesting in the area. This species, which is often thought to be heavily dependent on riparian areas, does occasionally use dry canyons. Elsewhere this summer one was photographed in Slaughter Canyon, and in the past a nest was found at the base of the Big Hill in Walnut Canyon.

Blue-throated Hummingbird: One male was seen on June 13th in the area beyond Stop 14. This is about the seventh recorded event for Eddy County and the third for Carlsbad Caverns NP. The species is seen annually at Guadalupe Mountains NP and is probably a regular in Big Canyon between the two parks.

White-throated Swift: On June 24th, two White-throated Swifts were found at Stop 13. Because few nesting locations exist for this species, it would be interesting to know where the nearest nesting colony is located. The only known colony in the park is in West Slaughter Canyon in Window Cave about 7.2 km to the southwest. There are undoubtedly additional nesting colonies of this species in the park.

Gray Flycatcher: This species has been recorded as nesting in the Sacramento Mountains to the north and the Davis Mountains to the south. They occur regularly in the summer in low numbers in portions of the Lincoln National Forest and undoubtedly nest there. One was seen between Stops 7 and 8 on June 13th, but was not seen again on June 26th. This may be the first summer record for this species for Carlsbad Caverns NP.

Cordilleran Flycatcher (*Empidonax occidentalis*): This species was seen at higher elevation stops on the June 13th survey (Stops 1, 2, 3, and 11) and on June 26th (1, 6, 7, and 9). This species is limited in distribution in the Guadalupe Mountains, being found in more mesic drainages.

Gray Vireo: This species was found at lower elevation sites on this survey. On June 13th they were found in the canyon bottoms and slopes from Stop 12 to 14 and beyond. They were more

18

widespr ad on June 26th, being found from Stop 4 to 14. On the latt r survey, they were singing on the a ljacent dry slopes at stops earlier than recorded on the previous survey. On both occasions, several were found beyond Stop 14. Taking the maximum numbers into account, it seems there were a ninimum of six to eight pairs in the area of the canyon surveyed. This species is listed as t reatened by the New Mexico Depa tment of G me and Fish.

Plumbeous Vireo: T nis species was widespread at higher elevations in the canyon, being found from Stop 1 to 12 and then becoming very scarce beyond that point. The species was restricted largely t o the canyo bottoms and absent from the adjac nt dry slop s. A nest was found with an incubati ig bird and ggs (Photo 5) on June 13th for the first park breeding record for this species.

Photo 5. Plumbeous ireo on nest between Stops 10 and 11, Open Hollo v Gulch, June 13, 2003. First nesting record fo Carlsbad Caverns NP.

Cave S allow: This species was seen only once, on June 26th, beyo d the last survey point. The nearest nown nesti ig site is a Cottonwood Cave on the Lincoln National Forest about 9 km to southwe it.

Northern Mockingbird: As with the other surveys, this as one of t e most ubiquitous species. For som reason the numbers dropped between the first and second surveys; 17 were found on the first ne whereas only nine were found on the secon l.

Brown- eaded Cow ird: Only one was seen on this cou it. This cou it was in one of the areas most isolated from any livestock grazing.

North Double Canyon

North Double Canyon (NDC) is differentiated from the canyon immediately over the ridge to the south that is also called Double Canyon. Thirty-two species were found on this survey route.

Expectations

This is one of the more isolated portions of the park with little, if any, bird inventory work done in the canyon. In a review of almost all field notes from the New Mexico Ornithological Society (1962 to 2001), no mention is made of Double Canyon. Although the survey of the field notes is not complete, over 1,400 reports were found from Carlsbad Caverns NP from 1962 to 1995 and nothing from Double Canyon. No mention of the area was made in either Ligon (1961) or Bailey (1928).

With no prior information, there was little to go on in terms of what might be expected. This canyon is relatively close to McKittrick Canyon in which several species of interest are found and which might be expected to occur in the park. One of these is Elf Owl, which prior to this 2003 field season, had never been found in the park. Black-crested Titmouse (*Baeolophus atricristatus*) is known to occur in small numbers in McKittrick Canyon (but may only be seasonal) and has never been recorded in New Mexico. A third species, Hutton's Vireo (*Vireo huttoni*), is regular in McKittrick Canyon and has been found only once at Carlsbad Caverns NP.

Vegetation

North Double Canyon had a very interesting plant community with a lot of variety and the extremely bright, blood-red madrones (Photo 6). The first half of the canyon was broad with large benches often on both sides of the drainage. The canyon floor was populated with large expanses of sotol and some Apache plume. Ponderosa pine, Texas madrone, little walnut, and others occasionally grew in the canyon bottom, but were more frequent on the adjacent slopes. *Acacia* spp. was also present throughout, but not as common as in other canyons. Beyond Stop 8, Rocky Mountain maple became the dominant tree.

Photo 6. Texas madr ne between Stops 4 and 5, June 20, 2)03.

Survey Details

The survey in NDC was run on two occasions—once on June 20th a id again on July 3rd. Access difficulties make ru ning the surveys earlier impossible, but as many species nest into July, this did not seem to ham)er the findings.

On both surveys, the PI was accompanied by Donna Laing and Mike Woolman. The PI ran the bird sur ey route while Donna and Mike did other work in the cany)n; they provided information on other birds they saw while in the canyon. On both survey trips, the field crew arrived n the day b :fore the count and camped near Stop 1. On June 19th, the PI walked the route be ore running it on the 20th, setting out flagging and noting e ich site, and then returning to the cam)site after dark. At the conclusion of both count ;, the PI continued up the canyon past Stop 14 ind onto adjacent national forest to investigate vhat else might be in the canyon. Photos were taken on each)f the survey points (Appendix J).

Twenty-nine species including 145 individuals were found on June 20th (Table 2).The number of species)bserved dropped slightly by the second survey date, July 3rd, to 23 species, a decline of about 21%. The nu ber of individuals also dropped onl y slightly to 139, a decline of less than 3%. Although 29 sp :cies were found on the first survey, Great Horned Owl (*Bubo virginianus*) was noted only between stops. Four other species: Black-chinned Hummingbird, Cordilleran

Flycatcher, Violet-green Swallow, and Black-headed Grosbeak (*Pheucticus melanocephalus*) were found just beyond the end of the survey (Table 3).

Results and Discussion
Although there were no major surprises in species found, there were some species that one might have expected to find but were not detected (see comments below on select species).

Golden Eagle: This canyon seems ideal for this species, large cliffs, isolation, and opportunities for thermals. Very few rock squirrels were seen, however, which might indicate a poor prey base. In fact, no mule deer were seen on the four days spent in the canyon and very little sign of mule deer were noted.

American Kestrel (*Falco sparverius*): This species was found in upper NDC at Stop 10 both as the PI went up the canyon and later upon returning. A large dead ponderosa pine is located here and there may be a nesting site in the tree or in a pocket in an adjacent cliff. This species was reported by Bailey (1928) to nest in the Guadalupe Mountains, but no nests have been found since this report was published.

White-winged Dove: One nest with two eggs was found about 2.5 m from the ground as the bird flushed between Stops 11 and 12. Although this species may nest in low density in deciduous trees in many of the canyons, nests are rarely located. This is the first one the PI knows of away from Rattlesnake Springs.

Mexican Spotted Owl: The more narrow parts of the canyon would seem to be prime habitat for these owls. None were detected, but little time was spent after dark in the upper reaches of the survey when they might have been calling.

Gray Vireo: Gray Vireos were very common in the canyon bottoms and on adjacent dry slopes. Whereas they were more common in other areas surveyed during the summer of 2003, they still comprised a significant portion of the avifauna of NDC. They were found on nine of 14 stops on the June survey and 10 of 14 in July. Additional birds were detected between stops. An empty nest, found on June 20th between Stops 1 and 2, was the first nest found in the park; on July 3rd an adult was incubating the contents of the nest. The brooding bird was not disturbed but was surely incubating eggs (Photo 7 shows the nest).

As a very conservative estimate, a minimum of 10 pairs of Gray Vireo appear to be along the route surveyed. Gray Vireo is listed as a threatened species by the New Mexico Department of Game and Fish.

Photo 7. Gray Vireo nest between Stops 1 and 2, June 20. 2)03.

Plumbeous Vireo: P umbeous Viereos were detected on y at the upper reaches of the survey line and in more mesic areas.

Varied Junting: Tw) Varied Buntings were recorded on both survey dates. In June, a singing male wa; detected at Stops 1 and 3 and in July at Stops 1 and 4. They were not detected at higher elevatio is in the canyon. Probably a minimum of two pairs are along the survey route. Varied Bunting is listed as threatened species by the New Me ico Department of Game and Fish.

Discussion

Overall, 1,524 individuals from 50 species were detected on point counts, plus an additional six species were recorded between survey points or on scouting trips before or after the survey date. Active nests were found of White-winged Dove, Mourning Dove, Cassin's Kingbird, Gray Vireo, Plumbeous Vireo, Northern Mockingbird, and Phainopepla. Nest-defense, dependent young, or other strong nest-associated behavior was noted in Say's Phoebe, Ash-throated Flycatcher, Rock Wren, Bewick's Wren (*Thryomanes bewickii*), Blue-gray Gnatcatcher, Canyon Towhee (*Melozone fuscus*), Rufous-crowned Sparrow, Varied Bunting, and Scott's Oriole. Because of the time constraints of the survey, an aggressive search for nests was not possible. Hot, midday conditions generally were present at the completion of the survey, and the PI did not want to disturb birds unduly at that time of day.

The summer 2003 surveys added one species (Elf Owl) to the park's bird list, provided a second record (since 1943) of a species once thought extirpated (Montezuma Quail), and added to the knowledge of nesting species in areas of the park rarely visited, including two state threatened species (Gray Vireo and Varied Bunting). First nesting records of Gray Vireo and Plumbeous Vireo also were established. Comments on some noteworthy species follow:

Montezuma Quail: The single encounter this summer only adds to the intriguing history of this bird in the park. Does a viable population exist? This needs to be determined before any reintroduction efforts are made. Habitat seems to be available (Yucca Mesa, Guadalupe Ridge, benches in Open Hollow Gulch, and North Double Canyon), but this species is extremely hard to detect.

Yellow-billed Cuckoo: The presence of Yellow-billed Cuckoo in two dry canyons, and the nesting record from Walnut Canyon indicates this species may be using this "atypical" habitat more than is realized. This should be evaluated further, especially beyond the mid-June timeframe.

Elf Owl: In light of summer records of this species for the park (the first), additional work should be done to determine the status of this species in other parts of the park including late evening tape playbacks. The population in the Guadalupe Mountains may be a distinct subspecies and that status is currently under review.

Gray Vireo: In the relatively small areas surveyed in the park during the summer of 2003, a minimum of 42 probable nesting territories were located. This is probably the largest nesting group in the state of New Mexico.

Varied Bunting: Discussions with New Mexico Department of Game and Fish personnel indicated that probably only five or so nesting pairs of this species inhabit the state. The surveys in the summer of 2003, covering only a small portion of potential habitat, found at least eight probable nesting pairs. Another two pairs were known during the summer in lower Walnut Canyon.

Though not discussed in this report, the data was also collected by detection type, time, and distance bands (Appendix K), and entered into the computer application FLIGHT ATTENDANT

4 (www.fs.fed.us/pnw/bird-populations) (Huff et al. 2000). If future surveys are conducted, analysis could be conducted to compare data between years and between sites.

Literature Cited

American Ornithologists' Union (AOU). 2011. Fifty-second supplement to the American Ornithologists' Union Checklist of North American Birds. Auk 128:600-613.

--------. 1998. Checklist of North American Birds. Seventh ed. Lawrence, KS.

Bailey, F. M. 1928. Birds of New Mexico. New Mexico Department of Game and Fish. Santa Fe, NM.

Huff, Mark H.; Bettinger, Kelly A.; Ferguson, Howard L.; Brown, Martin J.; Altman, Bob. 2000. A habitat-based point-count protocol for terrestrial birds, emphasizing Washington and Oregon. Gen. Tech. Rep. PNW-GTR-501. Portland, OR: U. S. Department of Agriculture, Forest Service, Pacific Northwest Research Station. 39p.

Ligon, J. S. 1961. New Mexico Birds and Where to Find Them. The University of New Mexico Press. Albuquerque, NM.

New Mexico Ornithological Society Field Notes. 1962-2001. Published by the New Mexico Ornithological Society. Albuquerque, NM.

Pyle, P., and D. F. DeSante. 2003. Four-letter and six-letter alpha codes for birds recorded in the American Ornithologists' Union Check-list area. *North American Bird Bander* 28:64-79.

Appendix A: Bird Species Detected on Point Counts or Incidental Observations, 2003

Table A1. Bird species detected. Birds are listed taxonomically by common name. Source for common and scientific names: http://www.aou.org/checklist/north/; source for species code: Pyle and DeSante (2003).

Common Name	Scientific Name	Species 4-Letter Code
Scaled Quail	*Callipepla squamata*	SCQU
Montezuma Quail	*Cyrtonyx montezumae*	MONQ*
Turkey Vulture	*Cathartes aura*	TUVU
Red-tailed Hawk	*Buteo jamaicensis*	RTHA
Golden Eagle	*Aquila chrysaetos*	GOEA
American Kestrel	*Falco sparverius*	AMKE
Band-tailed Pigeon	*Patagioenas fasciata*	BTPI
White-winged Dove	*Zenaida asiatica*	WWDO
Mourning Dove	*Zenaida macroura*	MODO
Yellow-billed Cuckoo	*Coccyzus americanus*	YBCU
Great Horned Owl	*Bubo virginianus*	GHOW
Elf Owl	*Micrathene whitneyi*	ELOW
Lesser Nighthawk	*Chordeiles acutipennis*	LENI
Common Nighthawk	*Chordeiles minor*	CONI
Common Poorwill	*Phalaenoptilus nuttallii*	COPO
White-throated Swift	*Aeronautes saxatalis*	WTSW
Blue-throated Hummingbird	*Lampornis clemenciae*	BTHH*
Black-chinned Hummingbird	*Archilochus alexandri*	BCHU
Acorn Woodpecker	*Melanerpes formicivorus*	ACWO
Ladder-backed Woodpecker	*Picoides scalaris*	LBWO
Olive-sided Flycatcher	*Contopus cooperi*	OSFL
Western Wood-Pewee	*Contopus sordidulus*	WEWP
Hammond's Flycatcher	*Empidonax hammondii*	HAFL
Gray Flycatcher	*Empidonax wrightii*	GRFL
Cordilleran Flycatcher	*Empidonax occidentalis*	COFL
Say's Phoebe	*Sayornis saya*	SAPH
Ash-throated Flycatcher	*Myiarchis cinerascens*	ATFL
Cassin's Kingbird	*Tyrannus vociferans*	CAKI
Western Kingbird	*Tyrannus verticalis*	WEKI
Gray Vireo	*Vireo vicinior*	GRVI
Plumbeous Vireo	*Vireo plumbeus*	PLVI

Table A1. Bird species detected (continued).

Common Name	Scientific Name	Species 4-Letter Code
Violet-green Swallow	*Tachycineta thalassina*	VGSW
Cave Swallow	*Petrochelidon fulva*	CASW
Bushtit	*Psaltriparus minimus*	BUSH
Cactus Wren	*Campylorhynchus brunneicapillus*	CACW*
Rock Wren	*Salpinctes obsoletus*	ROWR
Canyon Wren	*Catherpes mexicanus*	CANW*
Bewick's Wren	*Thryomanes bewickii*	BEWR
Blue-gray Gnatcatcher	*Polioptila caerulea*	BGGN
Hermit Thrush	*Catharus guttatus*	HETH
Northern Mockingbird	*Mimus polyglottos*	NOMO
Phainopepla	*Phainopepla nitens*	PHAI
Spotted Towhee	*Pipilo maculates*	SPTO
Canyon Towhee	*Melozone fuscus*	CANT*
Rufous-crowned Sparrow	*Aimophila ruficeps*	RCSP
Black-chinned Sparrow	*Spizella atrogularis*	BCSP
Black-throated Sparrow	*Amphispiza bilineata*	BTSP
Hepatic Tanager	*Piranga flava*	HETA
Western Tanager	*Piranga ludoviciana*	WETA
Black-headed Grosbeak	*Pheucticus melanocephalus*	BHGR
Blue Grosbeak	*Passerina caerulea*	BLGR
Varied Bunting	*Passerina versicolor*	VABU
Brown-headed Cowbird	*Molothrus ater*	BHCO
Bullock's Oriole	*Icterus bullockii*	BUOR
Scott's Oriole	*Icterus parisorum*	SCOR
House Finch	*Carpodacus mexicanus*	HOFI
Unknown		UNK

*Four-letter codes that, because of conflicts, are not "1st-order" codes, see Pyle and DeSante (2003) for more information.

Appendix B: Plant Species Observed In General Survey Areas, 2003

Table B1. Plants listed alphabetically by common name. Source for common and scientific names: *http://plants.usda.gov/*.

Common Name	Scientific Name
Acacia	*Acacia* spp.
Algerita	*Mahonia trifoliolata*
Alligator juniper	*Juniperus deppeana*
Apache plume	*Fallugia paradoxa*
Banana yucca	*Yucca baccata*
Beargrass	*Nolina* spp.
Brickellbush	*Brickellia* spp.
Cane (walkingstick) cholla	*Cylindropuntia spinosior*
Canyon (Arizona) grape	*Vitis arizonica*
Gray oak	*Quercus grisea*
Heyder's nipple cactus	*Mammillaria heyderi*
Honey mesquite	*Prosopis glandulosa*
Lechuguilla	*Agave lechuguilla*
Little walnut	*Juglans microcarpa*
Mescal bean	*Sophora secundiflora*
Mexican buckeye	*Ungnadia speciosa*
Mountain mahogany	*Cercocarpus* spp.
New Mexico prickly pear	*Opuntia phaeacantha*
Oak species	*Quercus* spp.
Ponderosa pine	*Pinus ponderosa*
Soaptree yucca	*Yucca elata*
Sumac species	*Rhus* spp.
Rocky Mountain maple	*Acer glabrum*
Sotol	*Dasylirion* spp.
Texas madrone	*Arbutus xalapensis*

Appendix C: Survey Route Maps

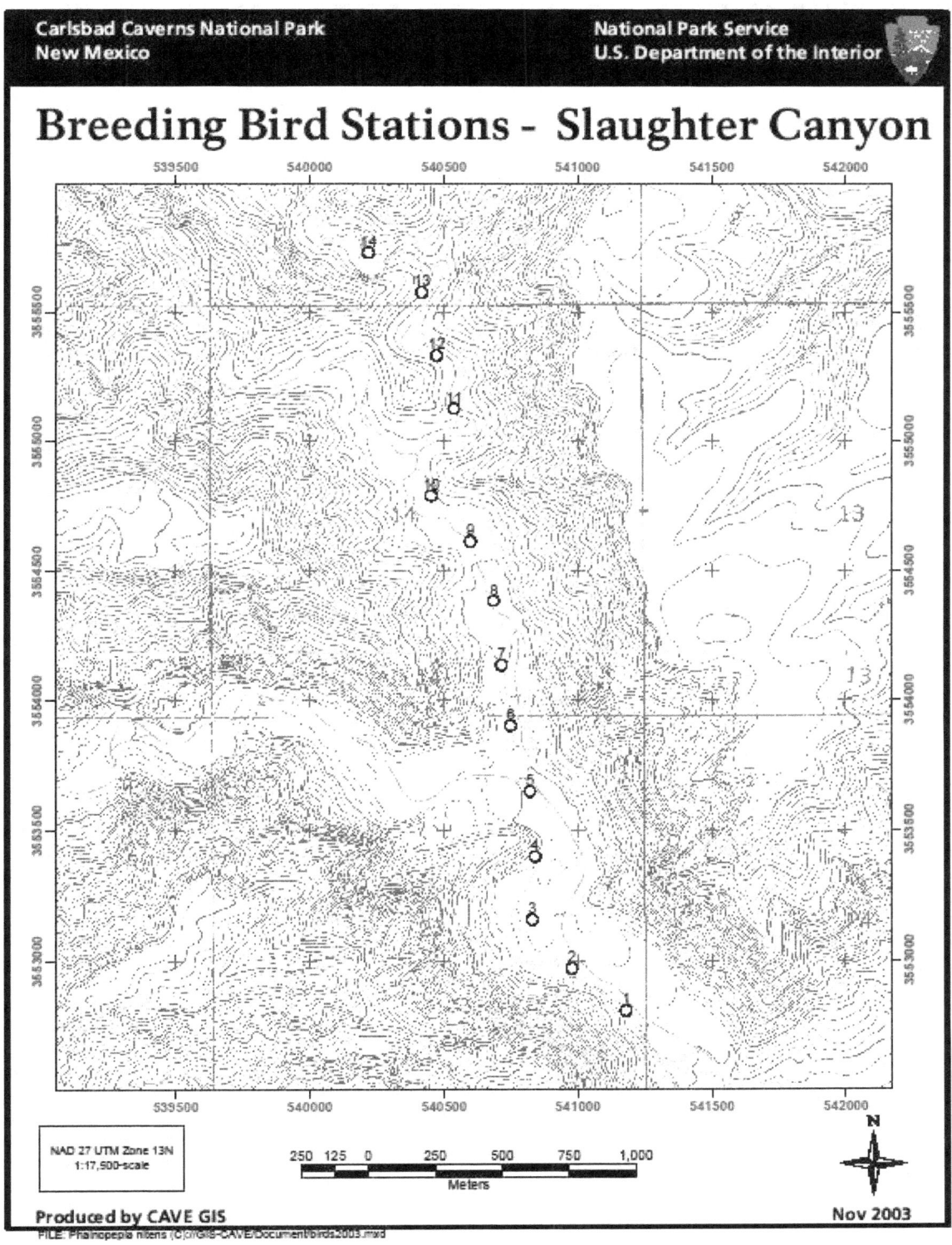

Figure C1. North Slaughter Canyon survey route.

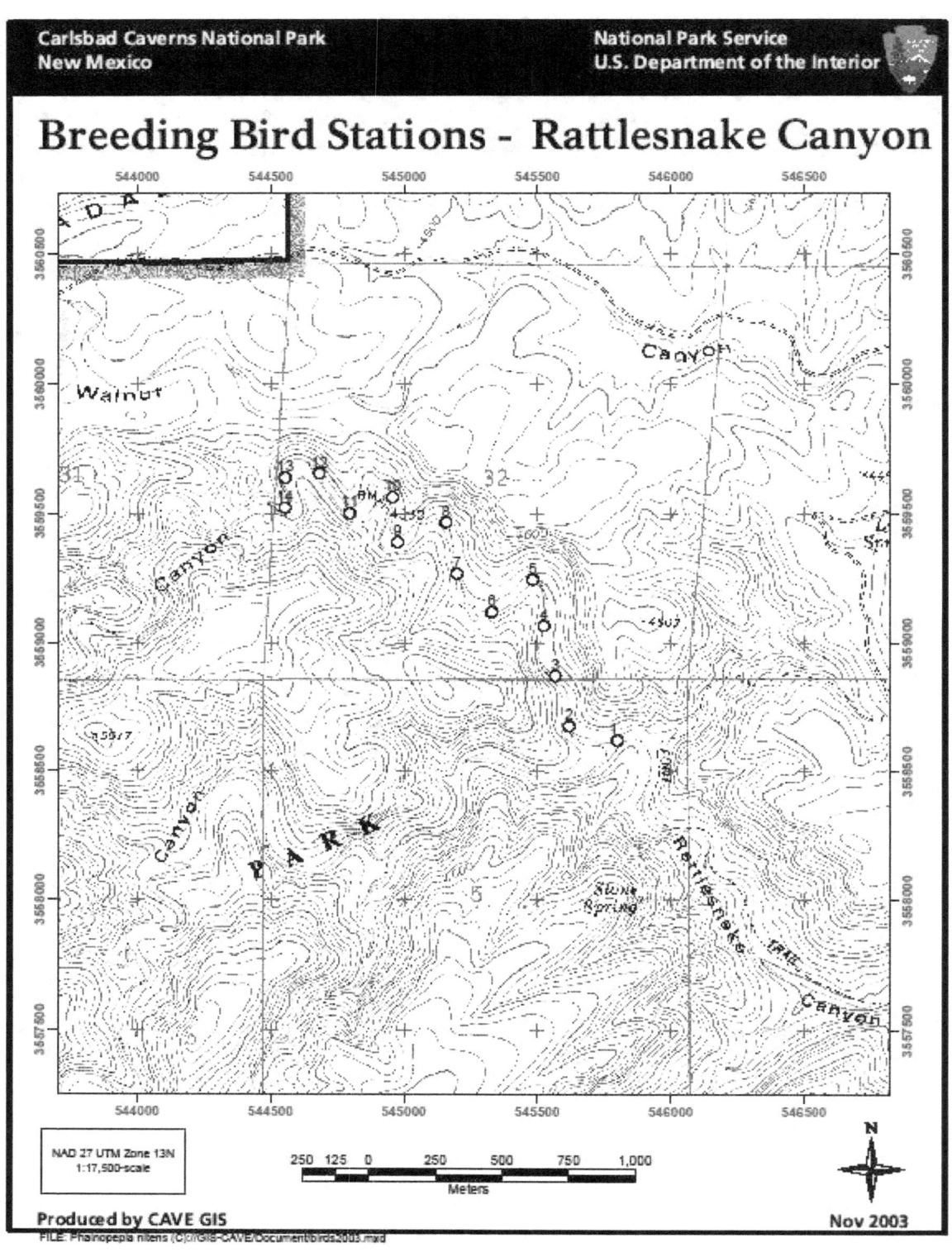

Figure C2. Rattlesnake Canyon survey route.

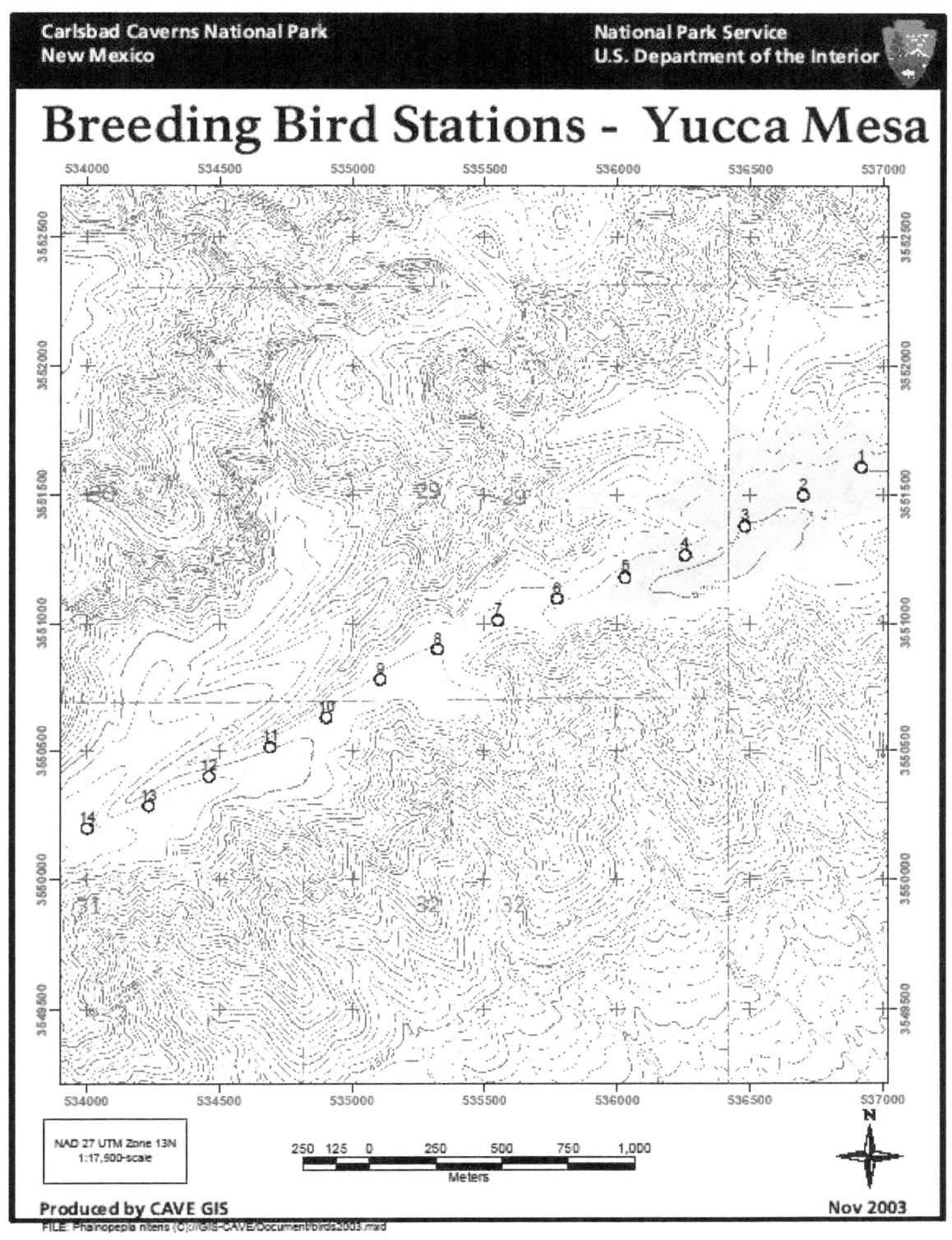

Figure C3. Yucca Mesa survey route.

31

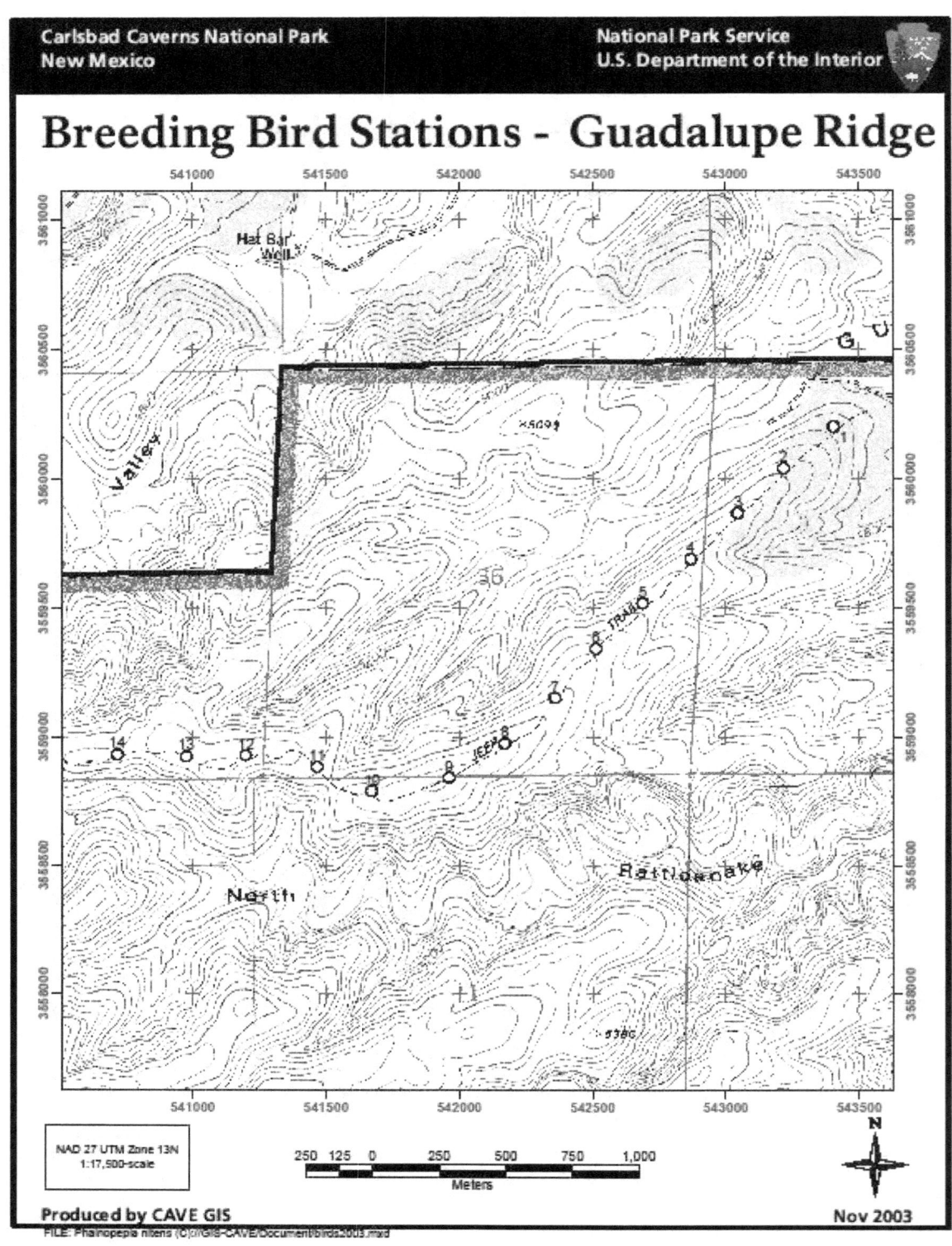

Figure C4. Guadalupe Ridge survey route.

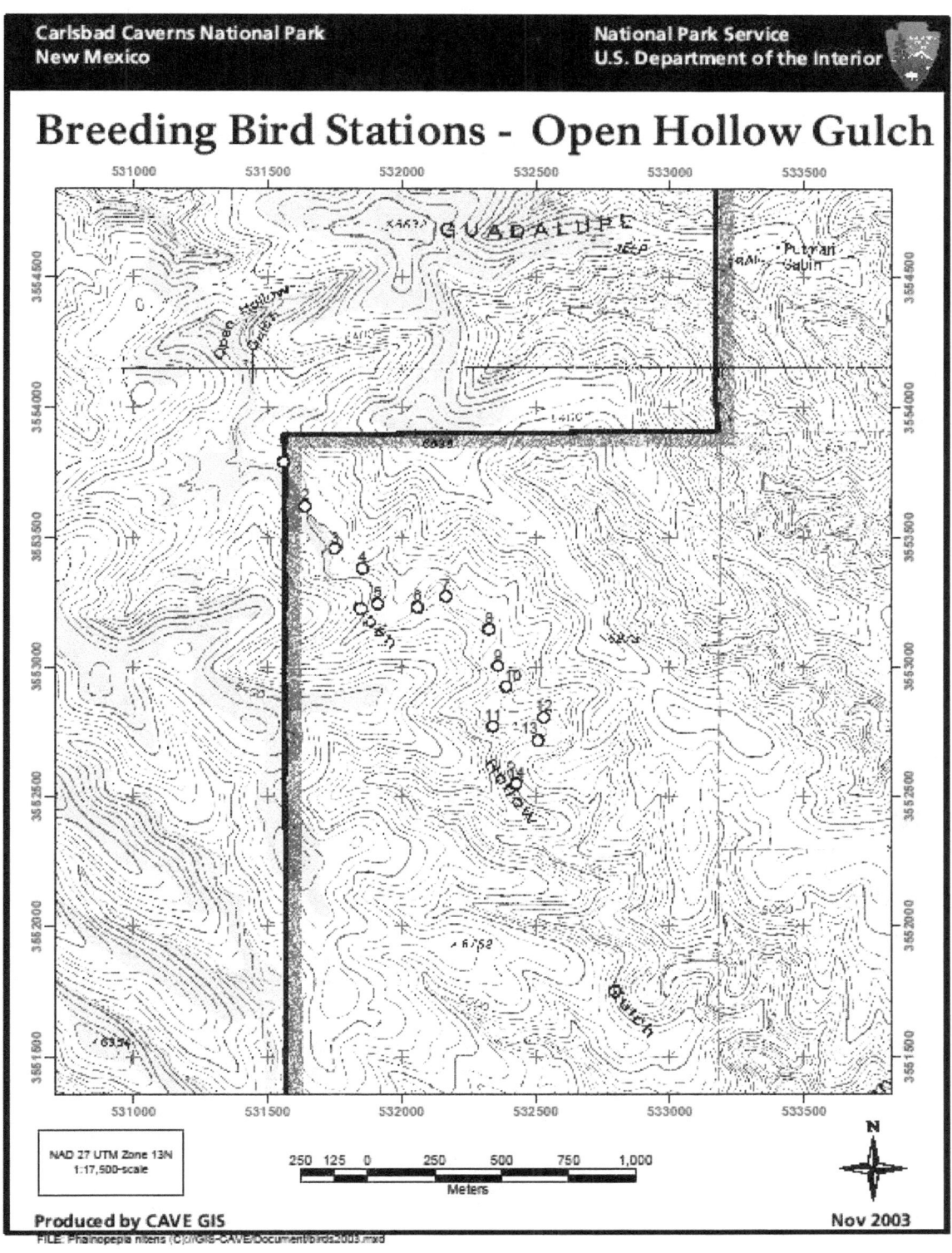

Figure C5. Open Hollow Gulch survey route.

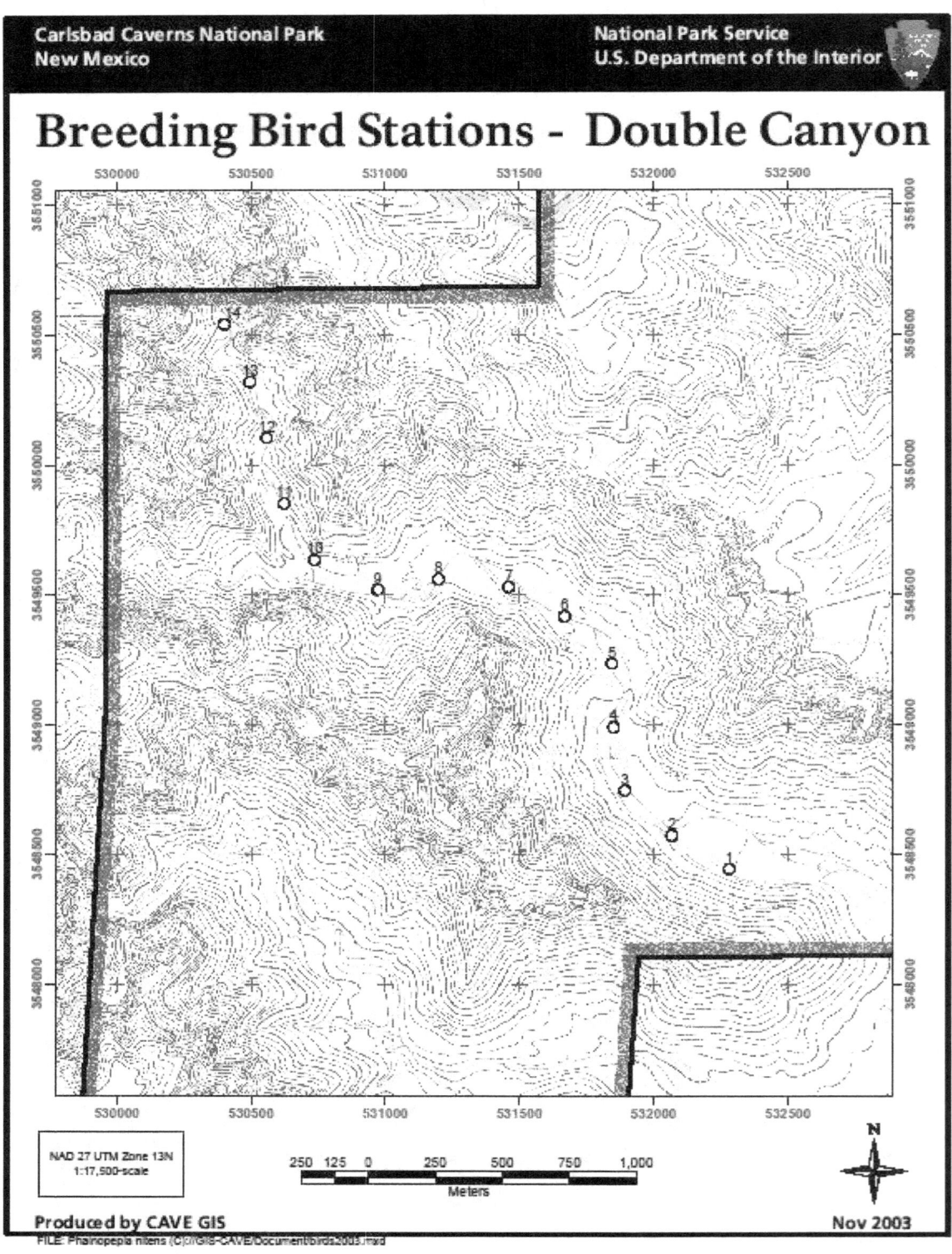

Figure C6. North Double Canyon survey route.

Appendix D: Point Count Locations

Table D1. Point count station locations, differentially corrected GPS, horizontal accuracy ±5 m; stations ordered by date GPS readings recorded.

Station	GPS Date	Elevation (m)	Northing NAD83 UTM	Easting NAD83 UTM
Yucca Mesa 01	6/2/2003	1819.67	3551807.82	536869.61
Yucca Mesa 02	6/2/2003	1828.23	3551699.64	536651.10
Yucca Mesa 03	6/2/2003	1829.41	3551579.46	536431.65
Yucca Mesa 04	6/2/2003	1824.47	3551468.60	536205.79
Yucca Mesa 05	6/2/2003	1822.43	3551381.67	535980.82
Yucca Mesa 06	6/2/2003	1815.94	3551299.40	535724.19
Yucca Mesa 07	6/2/2003	1817.04	3551214.06	535502.16
Yucca Mesa 08	6/2/2003	1822.10	3551102.11	535273.63
Yucca Mesa 09	6/2/2003	1825.17	3550982.22	535059.19
Yucca Mesa 10	6/2/2003	1827.22	3550834.48	534855.65
Yucca Mesa 11	6/2/2003	1836.39	3550720.35	534645.16
Yucca Mesa 12	6/2/2003	1842.84	3550603.91	534413.95
Yucca Mesa 13	6/2/2003	1849.81	3550489.32	534187.72
Yucca Mesa 14	6/2/2003	1864.07	3550402.87	533955.56
Guadalupe Ridge 01	6/6/2003	1479.33	3560404.96	543354.85
Guadalupe Ridge 02	6/6/2003	1520.97	3560243.84	543167.57
Guadalupe Ridge 03	6/6/2003	1540.10	3560070.61	542996.53
Guadalupe Ridge 04	6/6/2003	1562.98	3559892.17	542819.00
Guadalupe Ridge 05	6/6/2003	1581.13	3559721.87	542639.34
Guadalupe Ridge 06	6/6/2003	1618.50	3559545.53	542462.89
Guadalupe Ridge 07	6/6/2003	1632.31	3559357.37	542309.90
Guadalupe Ridge 08	6/6/2003	1661.01	3559179.27	542121.55
Guadalupe Ridge 09	6/6/2003	1680.65	3559045.81	541912.65
Guadalupe Ridge 10	6/6/2003	1674.74	3558992.53	541622.21
Guadalupe Ridge 11	6/6/2003	1658.54	3559087.63	541417.43
Guadalupe Ridge 12	6/6/2003	1678.24	3559134.15	541149.63
Guadalupe Ridge 13	6/6/2003	1680.79	3559129.84	540927.58
Guadalupe Ridge 14	6/6/2003	1656.92	3559136.03	540669.35
North Slaughter Canyon 01	6/10/2003	1284.37	3553013.41	541132.23
North Slaughter Canyon 02	6/10/2003	1290.23	3553174.48	540928.86
NorthSlaughter Canyon 03	6/10/2003	1296.43	3553359.76	540781.82
North Slaughter Canyon 04	6/10/2003	1305.58	3553602.89	540793.39
North Slaughter Canyon 05	6/10/2003	1308.07	3553850.11	540773.51
North Slaughter Canyon 06	6/10/2003	1315.64	3554103.07	540702.05
North Slaughter Canyon 07	6/10/2003	1330.06	3554338.51	540667.84
North Slaughter Canyon 08	6/10/2003	1331.65	3554587.16	540638.90
North Slaughter Canyon 09	6/10/2003	1340.45	3554817.58	540551.42
North Slaughter Canyon 10	6/10/2003	1346.91	3554994.10	540405.09
North Slaughter Canyon 11	6/10/2003	1364.62	3555329.17	540489.67
North Slaughter Canyon 12	6/10/2003	1377.84	3555534.71	540425.53
North Slaughter Canyon 13	6/10/2003	1396.97	3555775.93	540370.29
North Slaughter Canyon 14	6/10/2003	1411.53	3555928.58	540171.29

Table D1. Point count station locations (continued).

Station	GPS Date	Elevation (m)	Northing NAD83 UTM	Easting NAD83 UTM
Open Hollow Gulch 01	6/13/2003	1843.50	3553992.33	531511.58
Open Hollow Gulch 02	6/13/2003	1834.50	3553822.89	531591.29
Open Hollow Gulch 03	6/13/2003	1829.07	3553660.25	531701.22
Open Hollow Gulch 04	6/13/2003	1821.20	3553583.32	531805.71
Open Hollow Gulch 05	6/13/2003	1814.37	3553447.19	531862.57
Open Hollow Gulch 06	6/13/2003	1808.05	3553433.76	532009.99
Open Hollow Gulch 07	6/13/2003	1804.88	3553476.15	532116.08
Open Hollow Gulch 08	6/13/2003	1798.02	3553349.13	532278.75
Open Hollow Gulch 09	6/13/2003	1789.87	3553207.26	532311.35
Open Hollow Gulch 10	6/13/2003	1791.00	3553125.36	532342.37
Open Hollow Gulch 11	6/13/2003	1784.95	3552972.15	532292.36
Open Hollow Gulch 12	6/13/2003	1775.68	3553006.72	532481.90
Open Hollow Gulch 13	6/13/2003	1777.01	3552919.02	532459.93
Open Hollow Gulch 14	6/13/2003	1770.46	3552750.60	532379.07
North Double Canyon 01	6/19/2003	1488.53	3548647.57	532232.75
North Double Canyon 02	6/19/2003	1502.76	3548775.59	532018.63
North Double Canyon 03	6/19/2003	1506.92	3548949.48	531842.94
North Double Canyon 04	6/19/2003	1517.28	3549195.08	531801.81
North Double Canyon 05	6/19/2003	1526.93	3549440.09	531795.16
North Double Canyon 06	6/19/2003	1537.23	3549621.35	531618.00
North Double Canyon 07	6/19/2003	1549.92	3549734.13	531411.42
North Double Canyon 08	6/19/2003	1560.90	3549763.72	531148.57
North Double Canyon 09	6/19/2003	1572.49	3549723.67	530922.54
North Double Canyon 10	6/19/2003	1580.69	3549837.47	530687.44
North Double Canyon 11	6/19/2003	1595.58	3550054.65	530573.82
North Double Canyon 12	6/19/2003	1608.17	3550305.73	530509.65
North Double Canyon 13	6/19/2003	1620.13	3550520.70	530447.46
North Double Canyon 14	6/19/2003	1644.83	3550742.82	530352.46
North Rattlesnake Canyon 01	6/30/2003	1253.00	3558825.98	545751.32
North Rattlesnake Canyon 02	6/30/2003	1255.09	3558880.56	545568.42
North Rattlesnake Canyon 03	6/30/2003	1268.18	3559075.95	545517.81
North Rattlesnake Canyon 04	6/30/2003	1271.70	3559269.41	545475.04
North Rattlesnake Canyon 05	6/30/2003	1281.60	3559447.40	545433.89
North Rattlesnake Canyon 06	6/30/2003	1285.05	3559322.43	545280.90
North Rattlesnake Canyon 07	6/30/2003	1287.56	3559470.50	545148.58
North Rattlesnake Canyon 08	6/30/2003	1292.83	3559670.09	545107.86
North Rattlesnake Canyon 09	6/30/2003	1306.63	3559593.11	544925.95
North Rattlesnake Canyon 10	6/30/2003	1313.97	3559765.52	544908.16
North Rattlesnake Canyon 11	6/30/2003	1318.85	3559703.99	544746.37
North Rattlesnake Canyon 12	6/30/2003	1327.65	3559856.79	544632.99
North Rattlesnake Canyon 13	6/30/2003	1334.57	3559840.87	544505.21
North Rattlesnake Canyon 14	6/30/2003	1344.45	3559725.42	544504.73

Appendix E: North Slaughter Canyon Study Area Photographs

Photo E1. Stop 1, North Slaughter Canyon, June 10, 2003.
Dominant plants included little walnut, sotol, and Apache plume.

Photo E2. Stop 2, North Slaughter Canyon, June 10, 2003.
Dominant plants included little walnut, sotol, and Apache plume.

Photo E . Stop 3, North Slaughter Canyon, June 10, 2003.
Dominan: plants inclu led *Rhus* species, New Mexico prickly ɔear, and *Acɔcia* species.

Photo E . Stop 4, North Slaughter Canyon, June 10, 2003.
Dominan: plants inclu led *Acacia* species, sotol, and New Mexico prickly pear.

Photo E ɪ. Stop 5, North Slaughter Canyon, June 10, 2003.
Dominan: plants inclu led Apache plume, sotol, little walnut. I: was near this stop on the return trip that a Texas antelope squirr ɪl and an Elf Owl were found. This was the first report of an Elf Owl for Carlsbad Caverns ʌational Par ɪ. The owl was flushed from a stand of little walnut.

Photo E ɪ. Stop 6, North Slaughter Canyon, June 10, 2003.
Dominan: plants inclu led lechuguilla, *Acacia* species, and *Juniperus* species.

Photo Ê. Stop 7, North Slaughter Canyon, June 10, 2003.
Dominant species included little walnut, *Acacia* species, banana yucca.

Photo Ê. Stop 8, North Slaughter Canyon, June 10, 2003.
Dominant species included little walnut, sotol, and *Brickellia* species.
(No landscape view photo was taken for this stop.)

Photo E ⅃. Stop 9, North Slaughter Canyon, June 10, 2003.
Dominan: species incl ⅃ded little walnut, Apache plume, and sotol.

Photo E10. Stop 10, North Slaughter Canyon, June 10, 2003.
Dominan: species incl ⅃ded little walnut, sotol, and New Mexico prickly pe ∴r.

Photo E11. Stop 11, North Slaughter Canyon, June 10, 2003.
Dominant species included little walnut, sotol, and Mexican buckeye.

Photo E12. Stop 12, North Slaughter Canyon, June 10, 2003.
Dominant species included sotol, various oak species, and New Mexico prickly pear.

Photo E13. Stop 13, North Slaughter Canyon, June 10, 2003. Dominant species included sotol, *Acacia* species, and cane cholla.

Photo E14. Stop 14, North Slaughter Canyon, June 10, 2003. Dominant species included sotol, lechuguilla, and *Acacia* species.

Appendix F: Rattlesnake Canyon Study Area Photographs

Photo F1. Stop 1, Rattlesnake Canyon, June 30, 2003.
Dominant plants included little walnut, New Mexico prickly pear, and *Juniperus* species.

Photo F2. Stop 2, Rattlesnake Canyon, June 30, 2003.
Dominant plants included little walnut, sotol, and mescal bean.

Photo F . Stop 3, Rattlesnake Canyon, June 30, 2003.
Dominan : plants inclu led various *Quercus* species, sotol, an 1 Texas mad one.

Photo F . Stop 4, Rattlesnake Canyon, June 30, 2003.
Dominan : plants inclu led mescal bean, sotol, and algerita.

Photo F . Stop 5, Rattlesnake Canyon, June 30, 2003.
Dominan : plants inclu led sotol, little walnut, and mescal bean.

Photo F . Stop 6, Rattlesnake Canyon, June 30, 2003.
Dominan : plants inclu led Rocky Mountain maple, mountain nahogany, a ld little walnut.

Photo F . Stop 7, Rattlesnake Canyon, June 30, 2003.
Dominan : plants inclu led sotol, various *Quercus* species, an I mescal bean.

Photo F . Stop 8, Rattlesnake Canyon, June 30, 2003.
Dominan : plants inclu led sotol, mountain mahogany, and little walnut.

Photo F9. Stop 9, Rattlesnake Canyon, June 30, 2003.
Dominant plants included *Acacia* species, Rocky Mountain maple, and sotol.

Photo F10. Stop 10, Rattlesnake Canyon, June 30, 2003.
Dominant plants included little walnut, sotol, and various *Quercus* species.

Photo F11. Stop 11, Rattlesnake Canyon, June 30, 2003.
Dominant plants included little walnut, various *Quercus* species, and sotol.

Photo F12. Stop 12, Rattlesnake Canyon, June 30, 2003.
Dominant plants included various *Quercus* species, sotol, and mountain mahogany.

Photo F13. Stop 13, :attlesnake Canyon, June 30, 2003.
Dominan: plants inclu led sotol, Texas madrone, and little walnut.

Photo F14. Stop 14, :attlesnake Canyon, June 30, 2003.
Dominan: plants inclu led Rocky Mountain maple, sotol, and little walnut.

Appendix G: Yucca Mesa Study Area Phot graphs

Photo G I. Stop 1, Yu ca Mesa, June 2, 2003.

Photo G 2. Stop 2, Yu ca Mesa, June 2 , 2003.

Photo G 3. Stop 3, Yu ca Mesa, June 2, 2003.

Photo G 4. Stop 4, Yu ca Mesa, June 2, 2003.
A single Montezuma !uail was heard giving its dawn song ju st before this stop.

52

Photo G 5. Stop 5, Yu :ca Mesa, June 2, 2003.

Photo G 5. Stop 7, Yu :ca Mesa, June 2, 2003.

Photo G 7. Stop 8, Yucca Mesa, June 2, 2003.

Photo G 8. Stop 9, Yucca Mesa, June 2, 2003.

Photo G). Stop 10, Y jcca Mesa, June 2, 2003.
Old mou ttain lion scat was found just beyond Stop 10 on June 29th.

Photo G l0. Stop 11, Yucca Mesa, June 2, 2003.

Photo G|1. Stop 13, Yucca Mesa, June 2, 2003.
Old elk droppings wer∍ found between Stops 13 and 14 on 29 June.

Appendix H: Guadalupe Ridge Study Area Photographs

Photo H1. Stop 1, Guadalupe Ridge, June 6, 2003.

Photo H 2. Stop 2, Guadalupe Ridge, June 6, 2003.

Photo H ৷. Stop 3, Guadalupe Ridge, June 6, 2003.

Photo H ৷. Stop 4, Guadalupe Ridge, June 6, 2003.

Photo H 5. Stop 5, Guadalupe Ridge, June 6, 2003.

Photo H 6. Stop 6, Guadalupe Ridge, June 6, 2003.

Photo H 7. Stop 7, Guadalupe Ridge, June 6, 2003.

Photo H 8. Stop 8, Guadalupe Ridge, June 6, 2003.

Photo H). Stop 9, Gu adalupe Ridge, June 6, 2003.

Photo H10. Stop 10, Guadalupe Ridge, June 6, 2003.

Photo H11. Stop 11, Guadalupe Ridge, June 6, 2003.

Photo H12. Stop 12, Guadalupe Ridge, June 6, 2003.

Photo H13. Stop 13, Guadalupe Ridge, June 6, 2003.

Photo H14. Stop 14, Guadalupe Ridge, June 6, 2003.

Appendix I: Open Hollow Gulch Study Area Photographs

Photo I1. Stop 1, Open Hollow Gulch, June 13, 2003.
Dominan: plants inclu led Rocky Mountain maple, mountain nahogany, a id sotol.

Photo I2. Stop 2, Open Hollow Gulch, June 13, 2003.
Dominan: plants inclu led various oak species, Rocky Mount in maple, and ponderosa pine.

Photo I3. Stop 3, Open Hollow Gulch, June 13, 2003.
Dominan: plants inclu led *Acacia* species, ponderosa pine, and sotol.

Photo I4. Stop 4, Open Hollow Gulch, June 13, 2003.
Dominan: plants inclu led Rocky Mountain maple, sotol, and alligator juniper. Shells from the snail, *Rabdotu dealbatus* also were found at this site.

Photo I5. Stop 5, Open Hollow Gulch, June 13, 2003.
Dominant plants included alligator juniper, Rocky Mountain maple, and so :ol. Elk tracks were noted between Stops 5 and 5 on June 13, 2003. A Yellow-billed Cu :koo was se :n between Stops 5 and 6 on June 26, 2003.

Photo I6. Stop 6, Open Hollow Gulch, June 13, 2003.
Dominant plants included mountain mahogany, Rocky Mountain maple, a id various oak species.

Photo I7. Stop 7, Open Hollow Gulch, June 13, 2003.
Dominan: plants inclu led Rocky Mountain maple, sotol, and ponderosa pine. A Yellow-billed Cuckoo was heard calling on June 13, 2003 between Stops 7 and 8. A recent deer kill vas found between Stops 7 and 8 on June 13, 2003.

Photo I8. Stop 8, Open Hollow Gulch, June 13, 2003.
Dominan: plants inclu led mountain mahogany, Rocky Mountain maple, a id Texas madrone. Between Stops 8 and 9 were several large tree trunks that had fallen i ito the gulch. All had very old workings of Acorn Woodpecker on them.

Photo I9. Stop 9, Open Hollow Gulch, June 13, 2003.
Dominan: plants inclu led Texas madrone, ponderosa pine, and sotol.

Photo I10. Stop 10, Open Hollow Gulch, June 13, 2003.
Dominan: plants inclu led mountain mahogany, alligator juniper, and sotol.

Photo I11. Stop 11, Open Hollow Gulch, June 13, 2003.
Dominan: plants inclu led ponderosa pine, banana yucca, and mountain ıahogany.

Photo I12. Stop 12, Open Hollow Gulch, June 13, 2003.
Dominan: plants inclu led sotol, mountain mahogany, and ponderosa pine.

Photo I13. Stop 13, Open Hollow Gulch, June 13, 2003.
Dominan: plants inclu led mountain mahogany, sotol, and Rocky Mountai ı maple.

Photo I14. Stop 14, Open Hollow Gulch, June 13, 2003.
Dominan: plants inclu led Rocky Mountain maple, various oak species, and sotol.

Appendix J: North Double Canyon Study Area Photographs

Photo J1. Stop 1, North Double Canyon, June 20, 2003.
Dominan: plants at thi; site included sotol, Mexican buckeye, and various oak species. The Gray Vireo nest was found on the left bank of this drainage between sto is 1 and 2.

Photo J2. Stop 2, North Double Canyon, June 20, 2003.
Dominan: plants at thi; stop included Apache plume, sotol, a id little walnut.

Photo J3. Stop 3, North Double Canyon, June 20, 2003.
Dominant plants at this site include Apache plume, little walnut, and sotol. About 10 m upstream from Stop 3 a shell of the snail *Rabdotus dealbatus* was found.

Photo J4. Stop 4, North Double Canyon, June 20, 2003.
Dominant plants at Stop 4 included sotol, Apache plume, and various oak species.

Photo J5. Stop 5, North Double Canyon, June 20, 2003.
Dominan: plants at Stop 5 included sotol, lechuguilla, *Rhus* species. The first Rocky Mountain maple of the survey was found in the canyon between Stops 4 and 5.

Photo J6. Stop 6, North Double Canyon, June 20, 2003.
Dominan: plants at thi; site included sotol, Apache plume, and little walnut.

Photo J7. Stop 7, North Double Canyon, June 20, 2003.
Dominant plants at this site included sotol, Apache plume, and little walnut.

Photo J8. Stop 8, North Double Canyon, June 20, 2003.
Dominant plants at this site included various oak species, beargrass, and sotol.

Photo J9. Stop 9, North Double Canyon, June 20, 2003.
Dominant plants at this site included sotol, Rocky Mountain maple, and mountain mahogany.

Photo J10. Stop 10, North Double Canyon, June 20, 2003.
Dominant plants included *Acacia* species, beargrass, and Rocky Mountain maple.

Photo J11. Stop 11, North Double Canyon, June 20, 2003.
Dominant plants at this site included various oak species, sotol, and Texas madrone.

Photo J12. Stop 12, North Double Canyon, June 20, 2003.
Dominant plants at this site included sotol, canyon grape, and Apache plume.

Photo J13. Stop 13, North Double Canyon, June 20, 2003.
Dominant plants at this site included Rocky Mountain maple, Texas madrone, and sotol. Dead shells of the snail *Rabdotus dealbatus* were found between Stops 13 and 14.

Photo J14. Stop 14, North Double Canyon, June 20, 2003.
Dominant plants at this site included sotol, mountain mahogany, and Texas madrone.

Appendix K. Species Detection by Tally Type for Each Transect

Table K1. Species detection by tally type[1] for each transect. Total birds detected were summed for both visits per transect. (Birds listed taxonomically).

SPECIES CODE	TALLY TYPE	NORTH SLAUGHTER CANYON	RATTLESNAKE CANYON	YUCCA MESA	GUADALUPE RIDGE	OPEN HOLLOW GULCH	NORTH DOUBLE CANYON	TOTAL
TUVU	a0	1	1	1				3
TUVU	a3		1		1	1		3
TUVU	i0	7						7
TUVU	i3	1						1
TUVU	m0			1				1
TUVU	m3				1			1
RTHA	a0				1			1
GOEA	a0		1					1
AMKE	a0						1	1
SCQU	m0	2	1		3			6
SCQU	m3	1	2		1			4
SCQU	t0	2						2
SCQU	t3	2						2
WWDO	a0	1						1
WWDO	m0	1	1				4	6
WWDO	m3						1	1
WWDO	t0						1	1
WWDO	t3	1						1
MODO	a0	1						1
MODO	a3	1	1					2
MODO	fl						2	2
MODO	m0	7	3	5	1	7	1	24
MODO	m3	3	2	3	1	10		19
MODO	t0	2	3	4		5	1	15
MODO	t3	3	1	2		5		11
YBCU	t0					1		1
YBCU	t3	1				1		2
GHOW	t3	1						1
CONI	a0		2		6			8
CONI	a3		1	1	2			4
COPO	m0			1			2	3
COPO	m3	2			1		1	4
COPO	t3	1						1
WTSW	a0					1		1
WTSW	a3				2		1	3
BCHU	a0	1						1
BCHU	m3			1				1
ACWO	t3			1				1
LBWO	a0		1		1			2
LBWO	a3		1					1
LBWO	m0	1	1	1		1		4
LBWO	m3		1	1		1		3
LBWO	t0	4	4	2	2	7	1	20
LBWO	t3	2	2			4		8

Table K1. Species detection by tally type[1] for each transect (continued).

SPECIES CODE	TALLY TYPE	NORTH SLAUGHTER CANYON	RATTLESNAKE CANYON	YUCCA MESA	GUADALUPE RIDGE	OPEN HOLLOW GULCH	NORTH DOUBLE CANYON	TOTAL
WEWP	m3					2		2
WEWP	t0		1			4	1	6
WEWP	t3			1		7		8
COFL	t0					10		10
COFL	t3					5		5
SAPH	m0			1				1
SAPH	t3	1						1
ATFL	a0				1			1
ATFL	m0	5	3	3	2	2	1	16
ATFL	m3	4			2		1	7
ATFL	t0	20	1	2		2	7	32
ATFL	t3	13	1	2			9	25
CAKI	a0			1				1
CAKI	a3					1		1
CAKI	m0			10	1	3		14
CAKI	m3			4	2	6		12
CAKI	t0			16		21		37
CAKI	t3			11		23		34
GRVI	m0	3	2	6		2	9	22
GRVI	m3	1	6	6	2	2	13	30
GRVI	t0	4	13	9		6	10	42
GRVI	t3	3	11	10		8	10	42
PLVI	m0					7		7
PLVI	m3					7		7
PLVI	t0			1		19		20
PLVI	t3					19		19
VGSW	a0			1		1		2
VGSW	a3			2				2
CASW	a0	7	1	4	2		22	36
CASW	a3	12		5			19	36
CASW	i3	10					1	11
CASW	t0	15						15
CASW	t3	20						20
BUSH	t3					2		2
CACW	m0	5						5
CACW	t0	5						5
CACW	t3	5						5
ROWR	juv		1	3				4
ROWR	m0		3	1	1		7	12
ROWR	m3		4	6	1	1	4	16
ROWR	t0	4	9	6	1	2	5	27
ROWR	t3	2	3	8	4	2	3	22
CNWR	a0						1	1
CNWR	m0	7	12	3			20	42
CNWR	m3	3	8	3		1	16	31
CNWR	t0	1	10			4	2	17
CNWR	t3	3	4			4	4	15

SPECIES CODE	TALLY TYPE	NORTH SLAUGHTER CANYON	RATTLESNAKE CANYON	YUCCA MESA	GUADALUPE RIDGE	OPEN HOLLOW GULCH	NORTH DOUBLE CANYON	TOTAL
BEWR	m0				1		1	2
BEWR	m3			1	1		1	3
BEWR	t0	7	5	7	2	12	18	51
BEWR	t3	5	5	4	2	16	11	43
HETH	m0		1					1
HETH	m3		1					1
NOMO	a0				1	3		4
NOMO	a3	4		1				5
NOMO	m0	19	19	19	20	7	6	90
NOMO	m3	12	13	11	22	4	5	67
NOMO	t0	31	40	21	13	10	2	117
NOMO	t3	24	23	19	17	11	1	95
PHAI	t0	2	1					3
PHAI	t3	2						2
HETA	a0		3			3	1	7
HETA	a3					2		2
HETA	m0		1	2	1	2	4	10
HETA	m3		1	1	1	5	7	15
HETA	t0			4	2	13	6	25
HETA	t3		2	1		11	4	18
WETA	t0					1	1	2
SPTO	a3						1	1
SPTO	juv						1	1
SPTO	m0					2	1	3
SPTO	m3			1		6		7
SPTO	t0					8	14	22
SPTO	t3	1				16	15	32
CANT	m0				1		2	3
CANT	m3		1		1			2
CANT	t0	2	1	2	2			7
CANT	t3			1	1		1	3
RCSP	juv						1	1
RCSP	m0				3		6	9
RCSP	m3		4		4		9	17
RCSP	t0	3	7	3	6	2	5	26
RCSP	t3	3	5	1	3	5	6	23
BCSP	m3			2			1	3
BCSP	t0			1		4	2	7
BCSP	t3					1	2	3
BTSP	m3	2	1		2			5
BTSP	t0	1	5		1			7
BTSP	t3	2	1					3
BLGR	a0	1					1	2
BLGR	a3	2			1			3
BLGR	m0	6	7	5	3	1	11	33
BLGR	m3	3	2	5	2		14	26
BLGR	t0	10	18	4	8	3	22	65
BLGR	t3	12	14	3	4	4	21	58

Table K1. Species detection by tally type[1] for each transect (continued).

SPECIES CODE	TALLY TYPE	NORTH SLAUGHTER CANYON	RATTLESNAKE CANYON	YUCCA MESA	GUADALUPE RIDGE	OPEN HOLLOW GULCH	NORTH DOUBLE CANYON	TOTAL
VABU	a0	1						1
VABU	m0						2	2
VABU	m3		1				1	2
VABU	t0	1	3					4
VABU	t3		3				1	4
BHCO	a0					1		1
BHCO	m3		2					2
BHCO	t0	1		1				2
BHCO	t3	2		1				3
BUOR	t3	1						1
SCOR	a0			1	1			2
SCOR	m0	8	10	1	1	2	11	33
SCOR	m3	9	6	4	3	4	11	37
SCOR	t0	14	13	11		4	10	52
SCOR	t3	16	6	6	1	3	12	44
HOFI	a0		5			3		8
HOFI	a3		1	1		1		3
HOFI	m3					2		2
HOFI	t0	11		3	1	4		19
HOFI	t3	7	1	2		1	1	12
UNK	a3		1					1
UNK	t3	1						1
TOTAL		428	356	299	174	394	434	2,085

[1]Tally type codes for point count data (see table below) used for distance banding, time banding, and detection type.

Table K2. Tally type codes for point count data.

TYPE	TYPICAL DETECTION				FLYOVERS				JUVENILE	FLUSH
DISTANCE	0-50m		>50m		ASSOCIATION		INDEPENDENT			
TIME	0-3 min	3-5 min	0-3 min	3-5 min	0-3 min	3-5 min	0-3 min	3-5 min		
CODE	t0	t3	m0	m3	a0	a3	i0	i3	juv	fl